BRIDGING
HEAVEN
& EARTH

A
RETURN
TO THE ONE

LEONARD JACOBSON

A CONSCIOUS LIVING PUBLICATION

BRIDGING
HEAVEN
& EARTH

Other books by Leonard Jacobson

Words from Silence
Embracing the Present

Introduction

It is with great delight that I offer this book to you.
It brings to me a very satisfying sense of
completion. *Bridging Heaven & Earth* is the third
and final book in a trilogy. The first two books are
Words from Silence and *Embracing the Present* and
although each of these books stand alone, it is
useful to read all three to receive the full message
that I have been called upon to share.
In 1981, I experienced the first of a series of
spontaneous mystical awakenings, which
dramatically altered the course of my life.
These awakenings have occurred approximately
every three years and have brought with them
profound and sometimes, startling insights and
revelations.
There are certain passages in this book, particularly
the revelations about Jesus, which differ from
traditionally accepted views. If these passages
offend you, then ignore them. There is so much
in the book that will assist you in your awakening
that it would be a pity to miss this opportunity
because a few pages clash with your pre-existing
beliefs.

Introduction

On the other hand, if you read these pages with an open mind, you might find yourself opening to a level of truth that exists beyond the world of belief. I also include in this book the sacred geometry revealed to me during the fifth awakening, which occurred in New York City in 1990. I am sure that you will find these pages interesting.

Bridging Heaven & Earth is a deeply mystical work.

It is not intended for your rational mind.

It speaks to your heart and soul.

It reaches into the deepest levels of your Being.

It addresses the dimension of you which is Eternal.

It is intended to awaken you.

I invite you to read this book carefully.

Meditate upon the words.

Allow your heart to open.

You are a beloved child of God.

Indeed, you are a champion of God.

At the deepest level, you are One with God.

It is time to remember who you are.

In the beginning is the end

Heaven on Earth

There is a world that exists
within the world we know.
It has existed in its perfect state
from the very beginning of time.
It is an invisible world waiting
eternally to be discovered.
It is God's world.
Heaven on Earth.
It is a world of extraordinary beauty.
A world of wonder and amazement.
A magical world.
It is a world which is Timeless.
Eternal.
Perfect.
It is a living world that reaches out
and relates to you every moment.
The trees, the flowers, the birds, the animals
and even the insects are all experienced as loving
friends sharing this perfect world with you.

Heaven on Earth ....

Everything is experienced as a Living Presence,
a divine expression of God.
This world I speak of is the body of God.
It is not a world of the imagination.
It is absolutely real.
I know it from my own experience.
I speak from my own authority.
I can show you the way
but I cannot take you there.
You must go alone.
God's world is real.
It is here now.
It is hidden within the world you know.
It is hidden within the world you live in.
And the doorway is within you.
In a sense, you are the doorway.

God is

God is One.
God is the One in the All.
God is the silent presence
at the very heart of all things present.
God is everything in existence.
There is nothing that is not God.
Even nothing is God.

God is present

God is real.
God is present.
Only when you are fully present
will you encounter the living presence of God.

God is within

God exists at the very heart
of silence within you.
When you awaken to God within you,
you will see God in everything outside of you.
Even the distinction between
what is within you and what is outside of you
will dissolve as you enter
into Oneness with God.

God is the creator and the creation

God is both the Creator and the Creation.
If you want to know where God is,
look to the creation.
Everything created is God.
Everything you can see,
hear, taste, touch or smell
in this moment is God.
To fully experience this moment
is to experience God.

God's world

God's world is the real world
of the present moment.
From God's perspective, it is limitless.
It includes everything in existence.
It is without boundaries.
It is the One.
It is the All.
From our perspective however, it is limited.
Our participation in God's world is limited
to that which is in the present moment with us.
It is limited to that which we can actually see, hear,
feel, touch and taste in the present moment.
At first it seems ordinary.
It is ordinary.
But if you remain fully present,
then that which is hidden within the ordinary
will be revealed.
Slowly and gradually, you will encounter
in all things present, the living Presence of God.
Boundaries will begin to dissolve as you move
from your limited perspective
to God's limitless perspective.
Your consciousness will open and expand.
You will find yourself in Heaven on Earth.

Two ways to be with God

There are two ways you can be with God.
You can believe in God or you can know God.
Believers in God usually see God as existing
outside of them and there is a tendency
to personalize God in order to believe.
Believers need a Jesus or a Krishna
to represent God.
They are functioning at the level of mind.
They believe in God but they
do not know God.
Those who know God tend to see
and experience God in everything.
They know that the source of their connection
with God is within them and that they enter
into God's world through the sacred
doorway of the present moment.
They are functioning at the level of Being.
It is only possible to know God
through direct experience.
There is a third possibility where the knower
and the known dissolve into perfect silence.
All that remains is Oneness.
Eternal Presence.
Eternal Is-ness.

The present moment

The present moment
is the doorway to the Eternal.
To awaken into the eternal dimension
of existence is the fulfillment of your life.
It is the completion of your soul's journey.

Two worlds

There are two worlds.
God's world,
the world of the present moment.
And mind's world,
the world of the remembered
past and the imagined future.
Both are vast.
But only one is real.

A friend

I am a friend and a guide.
I can guide you through the maze of the mind
and its endless chattering thought
to an inner place of deep and lasting silence.
This place is the silent presence of your Being.
It is your very foundation.
It is the source of true love and true power.
It is a place of silent prayer
where you stand before God
in total devotion and surrender.

The journey

A man dived deep within himself.
"Good!" said the guide.
He traveled through all the experiences of his life
and childhood until all the events of the past had
been recalled and returned to consciousness.
He could see where he had gone astray.
He could see where he had been damaged
and he was healed.
"Now I can be of service!" said the man.
"To whom can you be of service?" asked the guide.
"To those in need of healing," answered the man.
"Keep going," said the guide.
And so the man kept going.
He journeyed through past lives.
He saw who he had been and he was amazed.
He passed through psychic realms
and he experienced great interference
and disturbance from those who dwell there
who are less than fully conscious
and did not know who he was.
He was very nearly lost, forever to wander
the endless labyrinth of the mind,
like a dog chasing its tail or a man
relentlessly in pursuit of his own shadow.
But he trusted every impulse.
He turned over every stone.
And he found the way through.

The journey ....

"I have survived and now I can be of service!"
said the man.
"To whom can you be of service?" asked the guide.
"To those who are lost," answered the man.
"Keep going," said the guide.
"But I am afraid!" said the man
"Go through it," replied the guide.
"Will I survive?" asked the man.
"I do not know," answered the guide.
And so the man continued, through realm
after realm and dimension after dimension.
He experienced Adam, the first man.
He experienced the beast, before Adam.
He experienced Christ on the cross
and revelation after revelation.
He went beyond Christ into the realm of the Gods.
He saw beyond and understood all.
He entered fully into Heaven on Earth.
"I have seen through the limitations of the great
religions," said the man. "I have understood the true
meaning of the words of Christ. The truth about
Jesus has been revealed. The resurrection is now
complete. Now I can be of great service!"
"To whom can you be of service?" asked the guide.
"To all those in search of truth," answered the man.
"To all those who would see through the veils
of illusion!"

The journey ....

"Keep going," said the guide.
"But there is nothing before me," replied the man.
"Enter fully into nothing," said the guide.
"But to enter fully into nothing,
I will have to surrender all that I have gained
and all that I have learned," cried the man.
"I will have to surrender everything."
"That is correct," said the guide
"Will it be lost forever?" asked the man.
"Perhaps!" replied the guide.
And so the man entered into nothing fully.
He became full of nothing and he was nothing.
Love would arise out of nothing
and return to nothing.
Truth would arise out of nothing
and return to nothing.
The man held on to nothing
and so nothing would remain.
And at the very heart of nothing was God.
"When I am in nothing, God is in everything,"
said the man. "I have found God and now
I can truly be of service."
"To whom can you be of service?" asked the guide.
"To God, of course!" replied the man.
"Good! " said the guide. "Now you may rest."

Three questions

There are three questions
which are of tremendous value
to those who are ready to awaken.
The three questions are:
Who am I?
Where am I?
What am I doing here?
The answers to these questions
will help you to find your way home.

Who am I?

At the very deepest level,
I am Pure Consciousness.
I am Pure Consciousness
without form and
without content.
The Pure Consciousness I speak of is not
unlike the space which makes up the universe.
Space exists.
It is formless.
It is infinite.
It is ever present.
Stars are born and stars die and yet space remains.
Planets come, planets go and yet space remains.
Everything is born, everything dies
and yet space remains.
Eternal.
Unchanging.
Unaffected.
At the deepest level, you are like this.
This is who you are.

Who am I? ....

You are Pure Consciousness.
You are Silent Presence.
Experiences come.
Experiences go.
And yet, at the deepest level of your Being,
you remain silent, unchanging, unaffected.
Feelings arise.
Feelings subside.
And yet at the deepest level,
you remain silent, unchanging, unaffected.
The years come and the years go
and yet at the deepest level,
you remain silent, unchanging, unaffected.
Lifetimes come.
Lifetimes go.
And yet at the deepest level,
you remain silent, unchanging, unaffected.
To know yourself at the deepest level
is to know yourself as Eternal.
To know yourself at the deepest level is to know
yourself as the Pure Consciousness of God.

Where am I?

At the deepest level,
I am pure consciousness.
I am silent presence.
But where am I?
There are two possibilities.
Either I am in the present moment
in the consciousness of Being,
or I am in the mind.
When I am in the consciousness of Being,
I am in the real world of the present moment.
I am fully present, relating in the moment
to that which is present with me.
I am in God's world.
When I am in the mind, I am not present.
I am somewhere in the remembered past
or the imagined future. I am in a world
of thought, memory and imagination.
I am in a world of ideas, concepts, opinions
and beliefs.
I am in the world of my thinking mind.
I am not here now and what I am
experiencing is not real.
It is illusion.
If I believe that it is real,
then I am lost in a world of illusion.

What am I doing here?

I am here to awaken from mind to Being.
I am here to awaken out of the past
and future into the present.
I am here to awaken out of fear into Love.
I am here to awaken out of the illusion
of separation into the experience
of Oneness with God.

Coming home

My true home is the world
of the present moment.
When I am fully present,
in an open and expanded state
of unconditional love and acceptance,
then I am at home.
I am at home in the Garden of Eden.
I am at home in Heaven on Earth.
I am at home with God.

The sole purpose in being here is to be here.

The soul purpose in being here is to be here.

Entering the present

Each moment you have a choice.
Will you be in the present moment
in the truth of life or will you be in
the illusory world of your thinking mind?
With gentle remembering,
you can choose to be present.
There is a key to being present.
You cannot be present in abstraction.
You can only be present in relationship
to that which is already here.
Simply bring yourself present
with that which is present.
Your breathing body exists in the present moment.
It cannot exist anywhere else.
The bird's song exists in the present moment.
A tree moving in the breeze
exists in the present moment.
By becoming fully present with your breathing body
or with the sound of the birds or with the tree,
you bring yourself out of the mind and
into the present moment.
There is a simple principle at work here.
The mind, by its very nature,
exists within the past and the future.
It cannot enter the present moment.

Entering the present ....

So if you attune yourself to that which
is actually present, then you must come
out of the mind to do so.
The mind will have to fall silent.
Thinking will come to a halt.
You will come out of the past.
You will come out of the future.
You will become fully present.
There is no other possibility.
You are not trying to stop thinking.
You are not trying to escape from the mind.
You are not trying to become enlightened.
You are simply making a choice to be present.
You are free to make that choice.
A total absence of judgment is the key
that unlocks the doorway to Being.
And as the doorway to Being opens for you,
your mind will become silent.
Relax into the silence.
Deepen into Presence.
Enjoy all that God has to offer you
in this moment. Enjoy the fullness
and abundance of this moment.

The world of Maya

Life as you know it is based upon your memory
of past experiences, and your projections of those
past experiences forward into an imagined future.
It is life at the level of mind.
In a sense, it exists but only as illusion.
It exists as thought, memory and imagination.
It exists as concept, idea and belief.
It is the mind's world of the remembered past
and the imagined future.
It is an illusory sense of life and yet you have
come to regard it as the truth of life.
To the extent that you regard life
at the level of mind as the truth of life,
you are lost in the world of Maya.
You are lost in a world of illusion.
In truth, there is no life
outside of the present moment.
How can you breathe outside
of the present moment?
How can you hear the song of the birds
outside of the present moment?
How can you behold the beauty of the distant
mountain outside of the present moment?
It is impossible to live life
outside of the present moment.
If you want to do so, you will have to enter
into the illusory world of the mind.

The present moment is free of the past

When you are in the world of the mind,
your past experiences define you and
give you a sense of who you are.
This sense of who you are
is based upon the past and is very limiting.
It includes all those painful and fearful
memories from your childhood.
It includes all the hurt and anger you are
still carrying from your past.
It includes all the limiting beliefs about yourself
that were programmed into your mind in those
early formative years. It includes all the patterns
of control and strategies of manipulation you
learned as a child. It includes past experiences
of isolation and separation.
It is not the truth of who you are.
You can spend years in therapy to overcome
these limitations. You can pursue an infinite
number of spiritual paths.
You can meditate for twenty-five years.
Or you can choose to be present. Now!
All the pain and trauma of the past and all the
limiting beliefs about yourself dissolve as you
awaken into the present moment.
The present moment is utterly free of the past.
In the present moment, you are healed. In the
present moment, you are restored to wholeness.

Liberation from the mind

If you manage to attain liberation
from the tyranny and bondage of the mind,
then where will you be?
You will be in a state of perfect presence.
You will be in a state of perfect harmony.
You will be awake in the consciousness of Being.
You will be awake in the consciousness of One.
Where the inner is as the outer,
the above is as the below,
and the beginning is as the end.
Duality will be in perfect balance within you.
It is a coming together of the Mind of God
and the Body of God within you.
It is a coming together of Heaven and Earth.
In a state of perfect Presence, you are the bridge
between Heaven and Earth.

Perfect Presence

In a state of perfect presence,
the Pure Consciousness that you are
is fully present in your breathing body.
You are finely attuned through the five senses
to that which is actually here now.
Seeing through your eyes,
hearing through your ears,
tasting, touching or smelling,
you are brought into existence
in the physical realm.
The formless is brought forth
into the world of form.

The sixth sense

As you focus through the five senses and bring
yourself fully present with that which is present,
a sixth sense begins to awaken within you.
This sixth sense is the sense of knowing.
Knowing arises in the moment.
It arises out of silence.
You do not know how you know.
It does not even matter what you know.
You just know.
Knowing is a function of Being.
It is immediate and always available
in the moment.
Knowledge is a function of the mind.
It is of the past.
It has no life in it.
Do not convert knowing into knowledge.

As you enter into Oneness with God,
knowing arises within you
simply because God knows.

Fulfillment

As you spend more moments in Being,
and as you become more grounded in Being,
you will begin to feel full within yourself.
It is the only way to feel truly fulfilled.
To be fulfilled in the moment takes
so much pressure off the mind.
At the level of mind, there is a feeling
of emptiness, a lack of fulfillment.
This drives you to seek fulfillment but
you seek fulfillment outside of yourself.
You seek fulfillment in the future
and future fulfillment can never truly satisfy you.
The more you seek fulfillment in the future,
the further you will take yourself away from the true
source of fulfillment, which is the present moment.
When you are in Being, you feel full
simply because the present moment is full.
When you are in the present moment,
you are in the abundance of existence.
The bird's song will fill you.
The warmth of the sun will fill you.
The caress of the breeze will fill you.
The laughter of a child will fill you.
Your breath will fill you.
It is only this fullness arising
out of the moment, which can give
you a sense of fulfillment.

The essential nature of Being

When you have awakened to the level of Being,
you do not repress or reject.
You do not judge.
You do not project or disown.
You do not explain, defend or justify.
You do not analyze.
You are neither for nor against.
You allow. You love. You include.
You welcome. You accept.
This is the essential nature of Being.
It cannot be any other way.
If you are not acting in accordance
with the essential nature of Being,
then you cannot remain in the realm of Being.
It is not a judgment.
It is not rejection.
It is a simple ejection.
You cannot remain in Being
unless your words, thoughts and deeds
are in harmony with the essential nature of Being.
Being must eject that which is not in harmony
with its essential nature.
Our immune system seeks
to eject that which is foreign to it.
It is the same with Being.

The sacred and the profound

As you become more grounded in Being,
the experience of the sacred and the
profound becomes more ordinary.
Occasionally, you have powerful and blissful
experiences of God and Heaven on Earth.
But generally it is more ordinary than that.
The profound is very subtle.
It is hidden.
You have to be finely attuned to the
present moment and to the silent Presence
in order to maintain your conscious connection
with God in those ordinary moments.

In moments
of Perfect Presence,
I am.
And God is.
And the whole of existence celebrates.

The four aspects of God

Love.
Truth.
Power.
Intelligence.
These are the four aspects of God.
As you awaken,
you will begin to feel
the presence of God within you.
To your eternal delight,
you will discover
that these four aspects of God
are being expressed within you.

Visit with the Master

A man journeyed a great distance
to visit an awakened Master.
"How do I arrive at truth?" asked the man.
"By surrendering belief," replied the Master.
"How do I arrive at love?" asked the man.
"By surrendering fear and the illusion
of separation," replied the Master.
"How do I arrive at power?" asked the man.
"By surrendering control!" replied the Master.
"How do I arrive at intelligence?" asked the man
"By surrendering to God," replied the Master.

The true message of Moses

Moses ascended the mountain twice,
each time receiving messages from God.
On one of these occasions,
he received the Ten Commandments.
They were given by God as a set of laws
for a people who had not yet been delivered
unto the Promised Land.
For these people, the Ten Commandments
were necessary to introduce a moral code of ethics,
a set of laws to live by.
They were necessary to ease the suffering
of the people who lived at that time.
But when a Jew, or anyone else,
through direct experience of God,
awakens to the hidden world of God,
the Ten Commandments are no longer necessary.
They become irrelevant.
Universal laws then apply
and they are applied from within.
An awakened Being has no need of ethics
or moral codes. He or she is governed by universal
principles of love and a deep recognition of the
divine Oneness of all things.

The true message of Moses ....

An awakened Being always acts
with openness, honesty and integrity.
An awakened Being always acts with love.
It is impossible for an awakened Being
to act in any other way.
It is his very nature. It is her very nature.
On another occasion, the message received by
Moses from God was of an entirely different kind.
Just as Moses was about to descend the mountain
to liberate his people from bondage, he asked God,
"Who shall I say has sent me?"
God's reply is one of the purest messages
uttered in the spiritual history of mankind.
"Tell them I am that I am has sent you."
To one who is not awakened,
these words have no meaning.
But to one who is awakened, these simple words
"I am that I am"
take on a profound spiritual significance.
They are the Holiest of Words.
They are the purest declaration
of the Presence of God.

The law of abundance

If your focus is on the abundance
of God's natural world,
then your life will be one of abundance.
If you fail to recognize the abundance
that is already here and if you focus on what
you do not have, then you will create lack
and deprivation in your life.
The outer world is a reflection of the inner world.
If your inner world is filled with the love
and light and peace of God which arises out
of the Oneness of your Being,
then what kind of outer world
do you think will be manifested?

To those who appreciate what they already have,
more will be given.

Abundance of the moment

Surrender into the present moment.
The present moment is always presenting you
with infinite treasures which will fill you
with delight.
The sun setting over a distant mountain.
A bird soaring into a cloudless sky.
Waves lapping against the shore.
A river flowing.
A flower blooming.
The gentle glow of a full moon upon the ocean.
A child laughing.
A leaf falling.
A bird singing.
Thunder and lightning.
Two lovers walking by.
If you could open fully to all
that the present moment has to offer you,
then how full would you be?
Would you need to search into the future for
fulfillment? Would you have much interest in things
past? Open fully to the present moment.
Fulfill yourself now!

Abundance

Abundance is a feeling inside of you.
It arises as a result of being present.
The more that feeling of abundance
is within you, the more existence
will respond to you abundantly.
If you carry within you feelings of fear
and separation and the belief
that you can not have what you want,
then existence will have to respond
to you accordingly.

Celebration

Let your life be a celebration of every moment.
Celebrate all that the present moment
has to offer you.
Celebrate the abundance
and the beauty of God's natural world.
Celebrate that you are alive in this moment.
Let love and joy arise in your heart.

The law of attraction

Whatever you think or feel, you will attract into your
life. If you have negative thoughts or feelings,
even at an unconscious level, or if you act in a
negative way, you will attract that negativity into
your life. If you act unkindly, you will attract unkind
people into your life. If you try to limit others, it is
you who will be limited. If you are judgmental or
critical, you will attract judgment and criticism to
you. If you are angry or blaming, you will attract
angry or blaming people to you. It is an energetic
phenomenon. It is quite possible to attract to you
angry or blaming energy floating in the ether,
and so you end up carrying negative emotions
like anger, blame, hatred and rage which do not
even belong to you. On the other hand, if you exist
in a state of love and abundance, which is the
natural state of your Being, you will attract the
experience of love and abundance into your life.
If you are caring and kind and generous,
you will find many people being caring and kind
and generous towards you. If you are friendly,
you will attract friends into your life.
It is very simple. Like attracts like.
The deepest level of this Universal law applies to
the experience of God.
If you think, feel and act like God, you will
attract the direct experience of God into your life.

Beyond denial

By being positive, you will attract the positive into
your life. However, you must be very careful
not to encourage denial of negative feelings
in using this approach.
If there are negative feelings within you,
it is not wise to deny them and superimpose
positive feelings over them. This will not work.
The negative feelings still exist at an unconscious
level and will attract the negative, even though you
are consciously focused on the positive.
The correct approach is to bring to consciousness
all those negative feelings, thoughts and attitudes
that are functioning within you at a hidden level.
Do not be in denial of them.
Bring all these negative qualities
like anger, hatred, jealousy and greed
into the light of consciousness.
Own them. Identify them. Confess them,
at least to yourself and to God within.
Take responsibility for them.
They are an inevitable part of duality.
It is your denial of them that keeps
them locked within you.

Beyond denial ....

As you bring these things into
consciousness, they will begin to dissolve.
They will have no energetic force to
control you or overwhelm you.
You will come into a place of balance
within duality. Then you can move to
and function from that place within you
which is beyond the positive and the negative.
It is in the Oneness beyond duality that you
will encounter the true nature of love
and abundance.
You do not have to focus on it.
You are it.
It is a part of your essential nature.
In Oneness, only love and truth and beauty exist.
And they exist within you.
When you are in a state of Being,
the outer world will manifest as a reflection
of this rich and abundant inner world.
In the Oneness of Being, you will encounter
the abundance of God's natural world.

The law of forgiveness

Through the doorway of forgiveness,
you leave the past behind.
Through the doorway of forgiveness,
you are released into the present moment.
Through the doorway of forgiveness,
love enters your heart.
Forgive all those who have hurt you and seek
the forgiveness of all those you may have hurt,
either in this lifetime or any other lifetime.
By praying for forgiveness,
you release yourself from Karmic debt.
Pray for the complete healing of any wound or hurt
that others may still be carrying as a result of your
unconscious and unloving thoughts, words or deeds.
Pray for their healing and redemption.
Pray for your own healing and redemption.
Forgiveness cleanses you.
Forgiveness releases you.
Forgiveness redeems you.

The law of cause and effect

Whatever you are experiencing in your life now
is directly attributable to or caused by something
you thought, said or did in the past.
Everything you think, feel, say or do
now has an effect upon your future.
Every choice you make leads inevitably
to the consequences which follow.
In this way you are truly responsible
for your experience of life.
This is the law of cause and effect.

The law of Karma

Consequences inevitably flow
from your thoughts, words and actions.
Living with these consequences is the law of Karma.
You can live out your Karma in one lifetime or
Karma can spread out over many lifetimes.
If you have been cruel and controlling in a past life
you will incur a Karmic debt which will be reflected
in your soul's journey over many lifetimes, until that
karmic debt is extinguished or dissolved.
According to Karmic law, you will have to
experience what others have had to experience
as a result of your thoughts, words or actions.
If you have judged someone harshly, you will find
yourself being judged harshly. If you have been
rejecting, you might find yourself being rejected.
If you have been violent or abusive, you might find
yourself a victim of violence and abuse.
In other words, what you give out, you get back.
As you sew, so shall you reap.

The law of Karma ....

The law of karma
is not an imposition of punishment.
It is meant to teach you through experience
what it is like to be on the receiving
end of your cruel and unloving behavior.
This will ultimately lead to compassion.
It will reveal to you that your choices lead to
consequences for yourself and others.
You will begin to bring consciousness
to your thoughts, words and actions.
You will know that if you want to experience
love in your life, your thoughts, words
and actions will have to be loving.
Ultimately, the law of Karma
will lead you into one of the highest laws of life
which was expressed by Jesus when he said,
"Do unto others as you would
have them do unto you."

Karma

Karma is not necessarily a negative phenomenon.
If you have been loving, kind, generous and
compassionate, it will be reflected in the
unfolding of your life not just in this
life but in future lifetimes as well.
It will also be reflected in
other realms and dimensions
of your multi-dimensional existence.

Unfulfilled desires

Unfulfilled desires lock you
into the world of Karma.
If you have unfulfilled desires
at the time of your death,
you will be compelled to return again
and again until those desires are fulfilled.
And then new desires will arise
until you come to realize that all desire
leads you away from God
and the present moment.
To have an unfulfilled desire
is a subtle indication that what God
has provided for you is not enough.
In a sense, it is a subtle rejection of God
and the present moment.
You are saying to God that you are not satisfied.
You want more.
You will have to pursue your desires
until you finally come to realize
that God's world is so abundant
that nothing more is needed
and that everything is perfect as it is.

Completing the past

Do you have any unresolved issues with any
of the people in your life? Are there any conflicts?
Are there any old wounds or lingering resentments?
Are there any unfulfilled needs?
It would be wise to resolve
these things before you die.
Through the power of forgiveness,
you can complete and release the past.
Forgive those who have hurt you.
Seek the forgiveness of those you have hurt.
You can approach the person directly
and ask for forgiveness.
But if that is not possible or appropriate,
then the forgiveness can occur
within your own consciousness.
Just ask God to forgive you.
If you are truly sincere, you can release
yourself from any Karmic ties or debts.
The whole purpose of forgiveness is to release
yourself from the past and enter more fully into
the present. Why wait until just before you die?
Do it now!

The law of the One

God is One.
God is the One in the all.
There is but one God and that is God the One.
Everything in existence is of the One.
One who has awakened lives in the
realization of the Oneness of all things.
He or she lives in the experience
of Oneness with God.
One who has not awakened experiences
a life of separation and seeks to overcome
the separation by living in a world of illusion.

The law of Love

God is love.
If you want to experience
the living Presence of God,
you will have to live your life
with an open loving heart.
You will have to live a life
of selfless loving kindness.
You will have to come to know
yourself as Love.

Love is giving

Love is giving.
It asks for nothing in return.
Love is abundant.
It knows nothing of scarcity.

The need to be loved

At the level of mind, you are separated from the
source of life. You are separated from the source
of love. You are separated from God.
And so you are in despair.
You are afraid of being alone.
You want someone to be there for you so that
you will not have to feel alone and separate.
You want someone in your life who can
complete you and make you feel whole.
You want to be loved and accepted.
You want to be important.
You want to be special.
You want to be recognized.
You want to feel whole.
And so you find each other.
You fall in love.
For a while you feel whole but it does not last.
It cannot last. For you cannot find wholeness
outside of yourself. It is impossible.
The source of love cannot be found outside of
yourself. Sooner or later, love at the level of mind
must fail. You will be returned to your separation
over and over again.
Lifetime after lifetime.
Until you turn around.

The need to be loved ....

Until you look within.
Until you remember who you are.
You are a Being of love.
You are an aspect of God.
You are complete and whole within yourself.
It is only when you are in the mind's world
of illusion that you feel separate.
Be careful.
Be watchful.
Be fully conscious when you enter your mind.
Do not stray too far into the mind's world.
For if you do, you might get lost.
You might not be able to find your way back to
Being. You might not be able to find your way
back to the present moment.
This is what has happened to all of us.
We have become lost in the world of the mind.
Stay in the world of Being.
Stay in the world of the present moment.
Remember who you are.
You are a Being of love.
You are Love itself.

Love

Love at the level of Being is like
the full moon on a cloudless night.
It shines on all without discrimination.
It is soft and gentle.
It bathes you in its light.
If you withhold love or if you are discriminating
in the sharing of love, so that some are favored
and others are ignored, then you have taken
the pure love of Being, which is your very essence
and you have given it to the mind to use.
You have taken love into the world of duality.
You have invited hate to enter into your life
and become love's partner.

There is no greater power than the power of love.

Anger removes you from love.

The separation of hurt and anger

For many people, hurt and anger
have become hopelessly entangled.
It is impossible to feel and express anger
because the hurt gets in the way.
It is impossible to feel and express hurt
because the anger gets in the way.
The coupling of hurt and anger
is an unholy marriage.
They must be separated.
Take responsibility for the hurt
and the anger within you.
They are yours alone.
No one is to blame.
Identify the anger.
Feel it.
Express it responsibly and release it.
Feel the hurt.
Express it responsibly and release it.
This will clear a large space within you which
was previously occupied by the hurt and anger.
It will clear the way for you to deepen into Presence.
It will clear the way for you to deepen into Love.

The power of true decision

Most of us live in indecision.
We cannot decide what we want.
Or even worse, we are split in what we want.
A part of us wants to go forward.
Another part of us wants to go back.
A part of us wants to leave our job.
Another part of us is afraid to leave.
A part of us wants company.
Another part of us wants to be alone.
We cannot decide what we want.
And so we begin to feel stuck in indecision.
Our energy becomes blocked.
We have interrupted the flow of life
with our indecision. Life cannot give us
what we want because we do not know
what we want. Life cannot respond to us
appropriately because we are giving out
contradictory messages that are impossible
to respond to.
Suppose that you are walking down a road
and you come to a fork in the road.
If you take the left fork,
you will come to the beach.

The power of true decision ....

If you take the right fork,
you will come to the forest.
You sit there wondering which way to go.
You love the beach but you also love the forest.
You cannot decide and so you remain there.
You are stuck.
As long as you remain in indecision,
you will go nowhere.
You will enjoy neither beach nor forest.
Even if you walk to the beach,
you will still be thinking about the forest.
And so you haven't really arrived
at the beach at all. A part of you
is still at the forest and you are split.
All you have to do is make a true decision
and you will come into wholeness.
Your energy will unblock as the life force
begins to flow again.
You will get what you want.
When you make a true decision, the
outcome is assured. In truth, the outcome is
contained within the decision.

The power of true decision ....

If you decide to take the left fork,
just turn left and continue walking.
You will surely arrive at the beach.
Do not think about the right fork.
Forget about the forest.
Let your desire to go to the forest
dissolve completely.
When you are caught in indecision,
you are caught between two alternatives.
You are caught in two possible choices.
In other words, you are caught within duality,
which means that you are caught in the mind.
To decide means to cut away from.
A true decision results in a cutting away
from the two to the One.
With a true decision, you choose one
and the other falls away completely.
There is no lingering in the alternative choice.
A true decision brings you out of the mind
and into the present moment.
It awakens you and empowers you.
It is like saying to God
"I am here now. And I know what I want."
And God will be relieved.
Now God can give you what you want.

Complaining is the victim's alternative
to decision and action.

Aloneness

Being alone has nothing to do
with being physically alone.
To be alone means that you
do not have your past with you.
And so there is no future.
There is just the present moment.
The past has disappeared.
All the wounds and traumas from the past
have vanished without a trace.
All the limiting beliefs you have about yourself
and others have dissolved.
There is no energetic involvement
with anyone from your past.
You are here now, moment to moment.
When you are with others,
you are fully present with them.
You are not caught up in their past or their
future. They are not caught up in your past
or your future. You are both here now,
sharing this precious moment together.

The future is determined by the present.
The true future unfolds through
the present moment.

I am

Beyond existence and non-existence, I am.
Beyond Being and Non Being, I am.
Beyond form and the formless, I am.
Beyond the known and the unknown, I am.
Beyond life and death, I am.
Beyond creation and destruction, I am.
Beyond the beginning and the end, I am.
Beyond everything and nothing, I am.

The eternal dilemma of God

God is One.
God is eternal is-ness.
God is eternal presence.
God is the One in the All.
God is.
Everything is in God.
God is in everything.
God simply exists as everything in existence.
In God's original state, God exists as Oneness.
There is no separation.
The eternal dilemma of God
is that One cannot know itself.
One cannot experience itself.
To know oneself involves
both the knower and the known.
To experience oneself involves
both the experiencer and the experienced.
In Oneness, there is no separation
between the knower and the known.
Thus God exists eternally and yet
God cannot know or experience God's self.
God simply is!

The eternal dilemma of God ....

This is the eternal dilemma of God.
If God is to resolve this eternal dilemma,
then somehow God the One
will have to become God the two.
In other words, God will have to create
and enter into duality.
But how can that be accomplished?
God would have to divide.
It would be like splitting the atom.
Separate nothing from everything.
Separate the creator from the created.
Separate the knower from the known.
Separate the beginning from the end.
Separate the above from the below.
Separate the mind from the body.
Separate the present moment
into the past and the future.
And accomplish all of this in an instant.
This is exactly what happened.
It was an event outside of time.
It was an event that created time.
It was an event that would unfold through time.
And so the pure consciousness of God was divided.
That which had existed as One
now exists as two.

The eternal dilemma of God ....

Where the body and the mind of God
were One, now they are two.
Where the above and below
were One, now they are two.
Where the beginning and the end
were One, now they are two.
Where light and darkness
were One, now they are two.
Where everything and nothing
were One, now they are two.
But who would journey into the dual realms
upon behalf of God? Who would journey
from God as everything into God as nothing?
Who would journey from Oneness
into the experience of separation?
Who would enter into the illusion of time?
Who would journey away from God
in order to return to God?
The answer is that I volunteered
for such a journey, and so did you,
even if you have no conscious memory of it.
You and I left the Oneness of God's perfect
existence and entered into the realm of duality.
We entered into the experience of separation.

The eternal dilemma of God ....

We journeyed into darkness.
We journeyed into nothingness.
We journeyed into time.
We are servants of God in this journey.
Actually, we are the champions of God.
We were created in the image of God
for this purpose.
We are that aspect or expression of God
that seeks to resolve God's eternal dilemma.
Our task is to enter into and experience duality
and then find our way back to the Oneness.
But we have become lost within time.
We have become lost within
the illusion of separation.
We must awaken out of the past
and future into the present.
We must bring duality into a state
of perfect balance within us
if we are to find our way home.
It is time to awaken out of our dream.
It is time to return to the One.
It is in our return to Oneness
that God's eternal dilemma is resolved.
It is in our journey away from God
and in our return to God
that God experiences God's self in us.

●

In the beginning was the One.

God without form
The pure Mind of God

God   the One

God with form
The Body of God

In order to resolve the eternal dilemma of God, One would have to become two. God would somehow have to enter into duality. The original duality was God as form (the Body of God) and God without form (the Mind of God). This is the equivalent of God as everything and God as nothing.

God can never be less than whole. If there is a movement within the vertical plane, there will have to be a corresponding movement within the horizontal plane. This is expressed in the scientific principle that for every action, there is an equal and opposite reaction. Now duality has become multi-dimensional. Time has been created.

Because God cannot be less than whole, God must constantly keep moving into wholeness and balance. Once there is a movement in one direction, God has no choice but to complete that movement in its equal and opposite direction. This results in infinite and continuing expansion. This diagram is a representation of that expansion in one direction.

If we continue with the simple notion that every movement and form of God in one direction must be completed in its equal and opposite direction, then an interesting pattern begins to emerge.

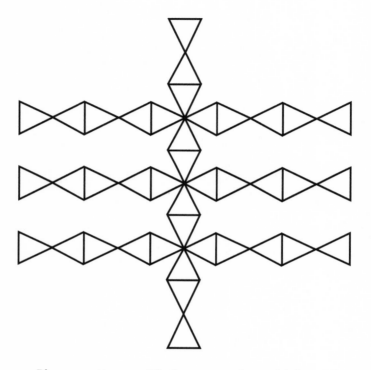

If we continue with the expansion which
we began on the previous page, a pattern
begins to form revealing the infinitely
expanding nature of God Consciousness

The pattern on this page expands infinitely.
It represents the perfect form and symmetry
of God Consciousness as God moves into
the process of creation.

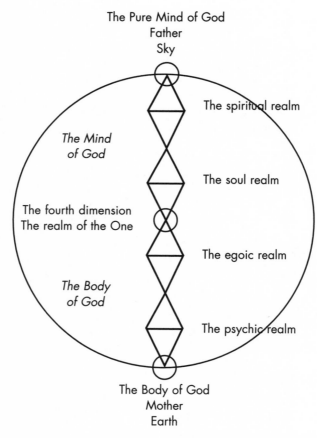

The Pure Mind of God
Father
Sky

The spiritual realm

The Mind
of God

The soul realm

The fourth dimension
The realm of the One

The egoic realm

The Body
of God

The psychic realm

The Body of God
Mother
Earth

In order to know God, God must be contained by a circle which limits the infinitely expanding nature of God consciousness. This circle of containment is human consciousness. It is a holographic part of the whole.

88

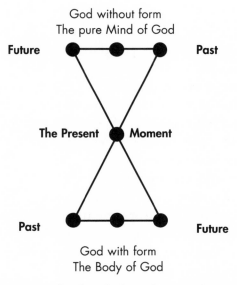

God without form
The pure Mind of God

Future · · · Past

The Present · Moment

Past · · · Future

God with form
The Body of God

Movement into duality led to the creation of time.
The movement into the realm above is a mirrored
image of the movement into the realm below.
Thus it can be said that, from a multi-dimensional
point of view, the past and the future exist
simultaneously but within different dimensions.
From the perspective of life lived in physical form,
if we open our consciousness into the mind of God,
which is formless, the upper realms of our
existence become available to us. Through the
doorway of the present moment, we can call forth
our own future, which already exists and is fully
evolved. We can call forth the highest and most
evolved dimension of ourselves.

The diagram on the opposite page represents the perfect balance that exists in the world of creation within time. The natural flow of energy in opposite directions holds the center perfectly in place. We create imbalance within duality, whenever we enter into rejection, attachment, judgment or desire. When we try to hold on to the past or control the future, we throw ourselves off balance. We disconnect from the center, which is the source and origin of our existence. We interfere with the natural flow of life within time. To understand the inevitability of enlightenment, even within the world of time, simultaneously follow the direction of the arrows in the diagram. Sooner or later, the multi-dimensional direction of time will lead you back to the Center. Sooner or later, you will be restored into Oneness.

If you relax, it is inevitable.

If you relax fully, it is immediate.

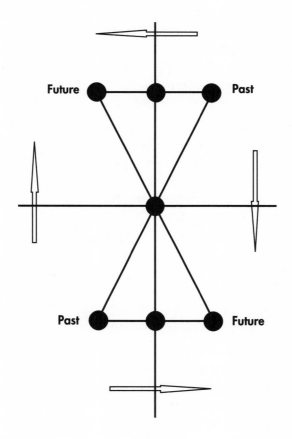

Separation from God

To the extent that you are lost and enclosed
within the world of the thinking mind,
you have entered into the experience
of separation from God.
You have entered into separation
from love and the truth of life.
The world of the human mind
is the realm of the ego.
It is a world of illusion created
by thought and sustained by memory.
It is a world of concept, idea, belief and opinion.
It is a world of the remembered past
and the imagined future.
It is not real.
But God is real.
God exists in the reality of the present moment.
God does not exist within an illusory world,
except as illusion.
By journeying into the human mind,
we enter into a world of illusion
and so we journey away from God.
We must return to the real world
of the present moment if we are
to encounter the living presence of God.

Journey of the Servant

By entering into the world of the human mind,
and becoming lost there,
you have journeyed away from God.
You have abandoned God's world
of the present moment for the illusory world
of the remembered past and the imagined future.
You have abandoned truth for belief.
You have abandoned the real for the unreal.
You have entered into separation.
You have separated from love.
You have separated from God.
But you are not guilty.
You have not done anything wrong.
You are the Beloved Servant of God journeying
away from God, so that you may return to God.
It is in your return, that God
will eventually come to know God's self.
It is in you that God's journey will be completed.
God will be restored to the One in you.
And you will be restored to the One in God.

You are the true hero.
You are the champion of God.

Ask God

I don't want you to believe me.
Ask God if what I am saying is true.
Close your eyes.
Bring yourself fully present
in your breathing body.
Bring yourself fully present
with any sounds you hear right now.
Know yourself as Silent Presence.
Know yourself as inner silence.
God exists at the very heart of inner silence.
Ask into the silence if what I am saying is true.
Ask God if you are the Beloved Servant of God.
Ask God if leaving God has been a part
of your service to God.
Ask God if you are judged or condemned
by God in any way. Ask God if you are much
loved by God for your service. Ask God when
your mission of service will be completed.
Ask God if it is time for you to come home.
And then wait. Be silent!
God's answer will arise out of the silence.
It may come in the form of a visual image.
It may come in the form of words
or it may come as a feeling.
And if no answer comes, then trust that.
Perhaps silence is the answer.

God is

In God's original state,
God exists as pure consciousness.
It is the consciousness of the One.
It is vast.
It is empty.
It is infinite.
It is eternal.
It is the source of all life.
It is the source of all light, love and joy.
It is Eternal Is-ness.
It is Eternal Bliss.

Everything and nothing

Everything and nothing is the original duality.
To know God as everything,
you will have to pass through the doorway
of God as nothing.
Beyond everything and nothing, I am.

At the very heart of nothing is everything.
At the very heart of everything is nothing.
When I am in nothing, God is in everything.

The present moment is the doorway to God.
The present moment is God.

A brief note to God

OK God, I get it!
You wanted me to leave the Oneness. You wanted
me to leave the state of eternal love and perfection,
where I was connected with all that is and you
wanted me to enter into Eternal Nothingness.
You wanted me to do this, even though I would have
to pass through an amazing experience of separation
which would be far too much for me to bear.
Nevertheless, you still wanted me to go off and play
the role of God as Nothing, whilst you play out the
role of God as Everything.
Somehow, in the separation of You as Everything
and You as Nothing, you get to resolve your eternal
dilemma and come to know and experience Yourself
through me.
There is only one problem, God!
Through the passage of time,
I have developed an ego and it is not very
happy with the role you have assigned to me.
It does not want to be nothing.
It wants to be everything, just like You, God,
and it is very committed to making itself
something out of nothing.
So there You have it, God.
The ego has had control of me for a long time,
but now that I know what You want,
how can I possibly refuse You?

A brief note to God ....

I can be nothing,
if that is what You want from me!
In fact, it is not that difficult.
I have noticed that if I bring myself
fully present with that which is present
(which of course is You in your role
as everything), my mind falls very silent.
Thoughts stop without any effort on my part.
The past drops away.
There is no future.
Things like blame and guilt and fear disappear.
There is nothing inside me.
Just pure consciousness.
A silent Presence.
I assume that this is what you mean by nothing.
But I must inform You God,
that it feels very full.
In fact, I feel full of nothing.
When I am fully present in this way,
I find myself overwhelmed by the beauty
of Your creation. I find myself overflowing with
love and gratitude. I find myself in a constant
state of awe and wonder.
To tell You the truth God, it feels and looks
a lot like Heaven on Earth right now.
Is this what you wanted?

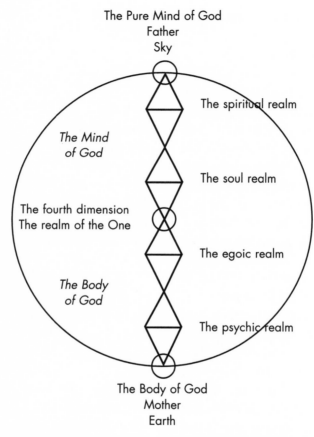

The Pure Mind of God
Father
Sky

The spiritual realm

The Mind
of God

The soul realm

The fourth dimension
The realm of the One

The egoic realm

The Body
of God

The psychic realm

The Body of God
Mother
Earth

In order to know God, God must be contained by a circle which limits the infinitely expanding nature of God consciousness. This circle of containment is human consciousness. It is a holographic part of the whole.

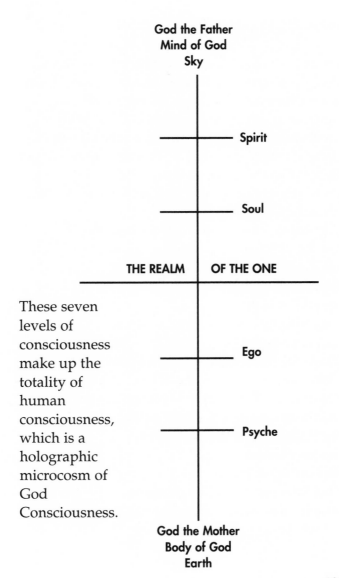

God the Father
Mind of God
Sky

Spirit

Soul

THE REALM | OF THE ONE

These seven
levels of
consciousness
make up the
totality of
human
consciousness,
which is a
holographic
microcosm of
God
Consciousness.

Ego

Psyche

God the Mother
Body of God
Earth

Realms of consciousness

There are seven levels of human consciousness.
Every human being living a life in physical form
is simultaneously living a life within all
seven levels of consciousness. Perhaps more
accurately, it can be said that all seven levels of
consciousness are living a life within each human
Being. Thus it can be said that our existence is
multi-dimensional even though we may not be
consciously aware of it.
The upper three levels of consciousness
are the divine realm, which exists as
the Pure Mind of God (Father, Sky),
the spiritual realm
and the soul realm,
which at the deepest level is eternal
and is an aspect of God or an expression of God.
These are the upper realms of human existence.
They exist independently of physical form.
The lower three realms of human existence,
are the divine realm, which exists as
the Body of God (Mother, Earth),
the psychic realm
and the egoic realm.
These are realms of consciousness
which exist within physical form.

Realms of consciousness ....

Each of these realms of consciousness
has its own laws and characteristics.
Each has its own purpose.
Each has its own limitations.
Each is a part of the whole.
There is another state of consciousness,
which I have not yet mentioned.
It is the fourth level of consciousness.
It is the realm of the One, the realm of I am.
There are three levels of consciousness above it
and three levels of consciousness below it.
It is in the center.
It is beyond duality.
It represents the coming together
of the two into One.
It represents the coming together of the past
and the future into the present.
It represents the coming together
of the above and the below.
It represents the coming together
of Heaven and Earth.
For most, it is a potential level of consciousness
rather than an actual level of consciousness.
The sole purpose of your journey is to realize
the consciousness of the One within you.

Awakening

Most of us are hopelessly lost
within the third level of consciousness.
We are dramatically out of balance
within the world of egoic experience.
Our journey is to awaken out of the illusory world
of the egoic mind and come to the center
within the third dimension.
It will open the doorway to God.
It will reveal the truth of life lived in physical form.
But even then, we will not be in the true center.
We are not just physical Beings.
We are multi-dimensional Beings.
We are spiritual Beings.
We are souls on a journey.
Most religions and spiritual traditions would have us
believe that the completion of our journey involves
ascension from ego to the spiritual realm.
This is untrue.
It denies the physical aspect of our existence.
It is a denial of the Body of God.

Awakening ....

To complete the journey, we will have to awaken
into that dimension of existence which includes
the physical and the spiritual,
the above and the below,
the past and the future,
the beginning and the end.
We will have to awaken into the
the fourth realm of consciousness,
the realm of the One.
The fourth realm of consciousness is inclusive of
all the realms of our multi-dimensional existence.
It is also transcendent of all the realms
of our multi-dimensional existence.
It is the Pure Consciousness of God.
It is the source of all life, light and love.
It is the One in the All.
It exists within you at the very heart of silence.
It is the purest form of love.
It is the truth of who you are.

Life at the level of ego

From the perspective
of our normal human existence,
we live within the third level of consciousness,
the realm of the ego.
We are lost within the world of the ego,
which is the world of the thinking mind.
The ego rules our lives and limits
our sense of who we are.
It is a kind of hell but we have grown accustomed to
it. We live in a world of thought, memory, opinion
and belief. In this world, we are both controlled
and controlling. The mind is constantly thinking
without any conscious intention on our part.
We have very little mastery over it as
it takes us into its world of the
remembered past and imagined future.
The doorway to the other dimensions of
consciousness is closed to us. We are denied the
direct experience of God in our lives. Instead, we
are condemned to live in a world of separation,
believing in God rather than knowing God.
Our world is a dual world and yet we are
dramatically out of balance within duality.
This keeps us away from the center.
It keeps the doorway to Oneness closed.
We must bring ourselves to the center
if we are to awaken into the truth of life.

Life at the level of ego ....

We can accomplish this by transcending
judgment and desire and by awakening out of
the past and future into the present moment.
This will lead to an awakened state of Being,
but to fully realize God consciousness,
the ego will have to surrender.
It will have to give up its control over your life.
It will have to make way for selflessness
and unconditional love.
It will have to surrender its need for
self-gratification and self-advancement
and allow you to live a life
of loving kindness and compassion.
To complete the journey,
you will have to awaken into the center,
which is the fourth dimension,
the realm of the One.
The doorway to the other realms will be opened.
Integration will take place.
Spirit will flow into your life.
The highest dimensions of your soul
will come forth into physical incarnation.
The Divine Mother and Heavenly Father
will come together as One within You.
The above and below will come together within you.
You will come into Oneness and wholeness.
You will begin to experience Heaven on Earth.

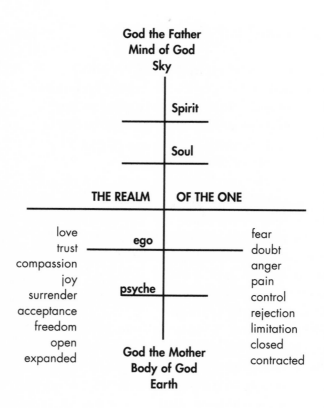

God the Father
Mind of God
Sky

Spirit

Soul

THE REALM | **OF THE ONE**

love		fear
trust	**ego**	doubt
compassion		anger
joy		pain
surrender	**psyche**	control
acceptance		rejection
freedom		limitation
open		closed
expanded		contracted

God the Mother
Body of God
Earth

Life at the level of ego is experienced within duality and within time. We must learn the art of balance within duality if we are to come to the center within the third dimension. We must learn the art of being fully present if we are to open the doorway to the realm of the ONE, which is transcendent of all duality.

Coming into the center

The first step in awakening is to bring
the dual world of experience within
the ego's realm into balance within you.
Through a transcendence of judgment and
desire you can come to that central point
which exists between
hot and cold, long and short,
happy and sad, joy and pain,
trust and doubt,
acceptance and rejection.
All experience exists within duality
including the experience of birth and death,
oneness and separation
and creation and destruction.
You cannot experience anything without
having first experienced its dual aspect.
In simple terms,
how can you experience acceptance
unless you have first experienced rejection.
How can you know happiness
without knowing sadness?
How can you know hot without cold?
It is impossible.
They define each other.

Coming into the center ....

You throw yourself into imbalance within duality
by becoming attached to the positive aspects
of duality or by rejecting the negative aspects.
Attachment and rejection are forms of judgment.
Judgment is the original sin which removes
you from the center.
Judgment leads to separation and creates fear.
As you transcend judgment in your life,
you will eventually be returned to the center
within the third dimension.
As you become more present and loving,
you will gradually awaken into
the fourth dimension,
the realm of the One.
You will find yourself fully present, with no
emotional or energetic involvement in the past.
At the very deepest level,
there will be no sense of your self from the past.
Separation will dissolve as you enter
into the Oneness of all things.
You will be overwhelmed with love
and compassion as you behold
the living presence of God
in all things present.

As above, so below

If you are to become established within
the fourth dimension in the realm of the One,
there will be both an ascent and a descent.
From the dimension of ego, an ascent occurs
as the ego surrenders and releases you
from the prison of the thinking mind.
From the dimension of soul,
there is a descent as the more evolved
dimensions of your soul enter into
and embody into physical life.
You exist in each of the realms
but until you awaken fully into Presence,
you do not exist in the center,
in the realm of the One,
which is transcendent of all duality.
Once you are firmly established in the center,
then the doorway to the other dimensions,
which was previously closed, will be opened wide.
Integration, balance and harmony will exist
between and within each of the realms.
This means that your soul will be delivered into
Oneness with God, which is the purpose of its
journey and the ego will relax and live a life
of joyful surrender within you.
Spirit will flow through you into the present
moment illuminating every aspect of your life.

Ego will not release you

Ego will not release you.
It has the doorway to the other realms closed.
It believes that if you ascend,
it will be abandoned.
It knows that it cannot come with you.
It exists in the past.
It cannot enter into the present.
It must remain where it is as it releases you
into the present moment which is the
doorway to Eternal Presence.
It must remain in the past
because that is its very nature.
It must remain in the third dimension
as it releases you into the fourth dimension.
It believes that it will be separated from you and
from God forever, with no hope of redemption.
It believes that it will be judged
and condemned to eternal Hell.
It must be guilty of some terrible sin
to deserve such a fate.
Many of our Scriptures reinforce this notion.
And so ego will not let release you.
It will not surrender if it means that it will be
abandoned into eternal separation from God.

Ego will not release you ....

It is too much for it to bear.
Who can blame ego for holding on?
If humanity is to be collectively released
from the bondage and tyranny of the ego,
there will have to be an end to judgment
and condemnation of the ego.
The ego has its place in your life.
It enables you to exist as an individual
within space and time.
It has its role to play in your multi-dimensional
existence, which crosses over boundaries
of space and time.
In its own way the ego is in service to God,
but the judgment that has been placed upon it,
particularly from the soul and spiritual realms,
has distorted its sense of who it is and the
true nature of its role in your life.
As you awaken fully,
the ego dimension of you will relax
as the patterns of control dissolve.
It will surrender and become your loving
and devoted servant, just as you
in a state of Presence, will be a loving
and devoted servant of God.

Spirit will not descend

Spirit will not descend
and flow into your life in physical form.
It believes that if it opens the doorway to
the lower realms, there will be a descent into hell.
Spirit does not know what is below it.
It can only know life in physical form
through your experience.
You convey the nature of your experience here in
physical form to the spiritual dimension
of yourself, through your feelings and emotions.
But what messages are you sending to the spiritual
realm? What message do you convey to Spirit with
your continual feelings of pain and hurt and anger?
What message do you convey to Spirit with your
feelings of fear and anxiety? What message do you
convey to Spirit with your feelings of helplessness,
depression and despair? What message do you
convey to Spirit with your feelings of greed,
competitiveness and jealousy?
As far as Spirit is concerned,
hell exists in the lower realms.
God exists above, not below.
Any descent would involve moving away
from God, and this Spirit will not allow.
Spirit has quite wisely chosen to keep
the doorway to the lower realms firmly closed.

False impressions

Spirit has no physical form.
It has no eyes to see the physical world
in which you live. It has no ears to hear.
It cannot taste or touch or smell the physical world.
You are the one walking upon the Earth.
You are the one with eyes to see and ears to hear.
Spirit has no way of knowing what life is like
in physical form other than through you.
But you are not truly here.
You are lost in a world of your own mind.
The impression of life conveyed to Spirit
is not an accurate one.
It is based entirely on the feelings and emotions
experienced within human egoic existence.
But those feelings are not a true reflection
of life in manifested physical form.
They are a reflection of a life lived
in the illusory world of the egoic mind.
Spirit has no way of knowing that you
are creating the whole experience of life
and emotions here with your imagination.
It is not real, but because you believe
that it is real, Spirit has no choice
but to believe that it is real.
And so Spirit will not open the door to the lower
realms. It has come to the conclusion
that it is hell down here.

Breaking a spiritual habit

In the spiritual realm,
we use the power of thought and imagination
to construct a sense of physical reality.
When we embody into the physical dimension,
we persist in using the power of thought
and imagination to construct our reality.
But we already have a body.
We are living in a physical world.
We are living in the body of God.
Everything in the physical world is the body of God.
There is no need for thought and imagination
to construct a physical reality.
But old habits die hard.
We cannot break this habit of using thought
and imagination to create the world we live in.
All that we succeed in doing is create
an illusory world of the mind,
which we are then condemned to live in.
We create our own personal world,
which separates us from the mind of God
and the body of God.
We must surrender this ancient addiction
to thinking and imagining and become
fully present in the body of God.

The descent of spirit

The completion of the journey
involves a descent from the spiritual realm
to the fourth dimension, the realm of Being,
the realm of the One.
This involves a descent from God
as Pure Mind into the realm of form.
Spirit will never allow you to descend
if it believes that to descend
is to leave Heaven and enter into hell.
Spirit has closed the doors to the lower realms.
It would take an earthquake to force them open.
You will have to find a way of communicating
with the spiritual dimension of yourself.
Let Spirit know that you have been in error.
Let Spirit know that you have been lost in illusion.
Confess that what you have been experiencing
is not real. Your emotional reactions at the egoic
level have had no foundation in reality.
You have been lost in your own personal mind.
You have been living in the remembered past
or the imagined future rather than in the present
moment. You have not been living in the
true reality of physical existence.
You have not been awake in the Body of God.

The descent of spirit ....

You have been lost in an illusory world
of your own creation.
This kind of communication will help Spirit
to relax and open the door.
Spirit has no body.
It exists within the Mind of God.
It knows nothing of Earth.
It knows nothing of the true physical existence.
If there is to be a coming together of Heaven
and Earth, then you will have to awaken out
of the mind into the reality of the present moment.
Only you can deliver to Spirit an experience
of the true nature of physical existence.
But you will have to transcend ego to do so.
You are the deliverer.
Once you are fully established in the reality of the
present moment, then Spirit will slowly
come to know the truth through you.
And then Spirit will flow freely into each moment
bringing with it the Divine Light of God
to illuminate everything in your life.

Calling to Spirit

Call out through the darkness to Spirit.
"I have been wrong! I have been lost!
I have not been living
in the truth of physical reality.
I have been lost in my own mind.
I have been lost in my own past.
I have been lost in an illusory world
of my own creation.
I have been defying God.
I have been competing with God.
I am sorry. I am truly repentant.
Please forgive me.
I am free now.
I am released from the prison of my own mind.
I am clear of the past. I am fully present.
I am the prodigal son returned home.
What I see now is the truth.
What I hear now is the truth.
Come Spirit. Come Soul.
Come Psyche. Come Ego.
Come Mother. Come Father.
Come One.
Come All.

Calling to spirit ....

Come into the body.
Come into the truth of physical existence.
Look through my eyes.
See the vastness of the sky.
See the silent splendor of a tree.
See the beauty in a bed of roses.
Come!
Hear through my ears.
Hear the song of the birds.
Hear the innocent laughter of a child.
Come!
Feel the breeze upon my face.
Let the mystery of existence
reveal itself through me in this moment.
For I am the One.
I am the one in the All.
I am above.
I am below.
And now I am established in the center.
I am that I am."

The coming together of Heaven and Earth

The Mind of God is Heaven.
The Body of God is Earth.
The final stage of the journey is the
coming together of Heaven and Earth.

I am the One

I am the One.
I am the One in the All.
I am that.
I am.
In me, the truth shall be known.
Through me, all will be revealed.
I an at the very center of your Being,
I am your foundation.
I am your rock.
Upon me, you may build your Jerusalem.

As you awaken

As you awaken into the fourth dimension,
there will be an end to separation
between the realms.
You will be living as an individual
existing within time but grounded in
the truth and reality of the present moment.
As the process of awakening deepens,
higher levels of the soul
will enter into physical form.
The spiritual essence of your existence
will flow into your life.
You will experience the Mind of God
as a vast and silent stillness
filled with endless light.
You will experience all things
in physical form as the Body of God,
radiant with the Living Presence
of the One True God.
You will experience the pure essence
of God which is Love.

As you awaken

As you awaken into Being,
the darkness of mind's world
will gradually become illumined.
You will have periods of intense illumination
which will dissolve all belief in illusion.
You will slowly but surely become enlightened.
You will come to recognize the truth of
who you are, where you have been,
and what you have been doing.

As you awaken

As you awaken,
the consciousness of Being
will bring all the qualities of
the Oneness of God into your life.
Silence, love, beauty, truth, power,
acceptance, peace, balance and harmony.

As you awaken

As you awaken, the consciousness of Being
will bring with it a gradual revelation of truth.
First about yourself and your life,
then about your past lives
and then about the spiritual and soul
levels of your existence.
It also brings with it revelation about the
collective levels of human consciousness.
Finally it brings divine revelation
about Buddha, Krishna, Christ,
God and the Eternal realms.

A loud round of applause

To come to the center
within the fourth dimension
is the completion of the soul's journey.
It is the coming together of Heaven and Earth.
In you, God is restored to the Center.
In you, God is restored to the One.
It is an event that will be celebrated
throughout the invisible realms.
Even though you may not hear it,
there will be a loud round of applause
which can only be heard in Heaven.

There is nothing you can do

There is nothing you can do.
Just relax.
Trust.
Allow life to unfold within you.
Allow God to unfold within you.

I come from the Sky

I come from the Sky.
From God who is my Father.
I go to the Earth.
To God who is my Mother.
I come from the end and I go to the beginning.
I come from the beginning and I go to the end.
I do this over and over again
until I come to rest in the center.
Between the beginning and the end.
Between the sky and the earth.
Between the Mother and the Father.
I am a child of God.
I am a servant of God.
I am the restorer of God.
I am the bridge between Heaven and Earth.
In me, God is restored to the One.

The dreamtime

Somewhere in our divine origins,
we existed as the Divine Family.
We lived in God's world.
A perfect world.
We lived as God the Mother.
And God the Father.
We had a son and a daughter.
We existed in perfect harmony,
living in a timeless land.
It was a Paradise.
A Garden of Eden.
A land of love and eternal beauty.
A land of endless wonder.
There was no sense of separation.
We were One.
Mother, father, daughter, son.
A perfect reflection of the Oneness of God.
There was no aging and there was no death,
because there was no time.
Our children would be our children forever.
They were innocent.
And they were beautiful.
Suddenly our perfect lives were shaken.
We were about to experience the separation.

The dreamtime ....

Our children were about to enter time.
It was the beginning
of the end of their childhood.
They had chosen to grow.
To mature.
To stand alone.
To go their own way.
In order to grow,
they would have to enter a dimension
where growth and change was possible.
They would have to enter the mind.
They would have to enter time.
Growth can only take place within time.
Growth can only occur within the mind.
It is a world of illusion but there is no other way.
They had chosen their path.
They had entered the mind.
And they were lost to us.
We awaited their return but they did not return.
They could not return.
For ours is an eternal realm without change
and they had chosen to change.
They could never return as our children.
How we loved them.

The dreamtime ....

How we longed for them.
If we were to be with them again,
we would have to find them.
We would have to follow them into the mind.
We would have to follow them into time.
And so we journeyed into time.
Driven by the memory of our lost children,
we entered the mind.
We had never been there before
and very soon, we were lost.
Before we could find our children,
they had grown old and they had died.
They entered into the soul's realm,
which is an intermediate realm.
They were not meant to linger there,
but from the soul's realm,
they could see what had happened to us.
They could see that we had tried to
find them and that we had lost our way.
They entered again as children in order to find us.
Before they could find us,
we had grown old and we had died.
We chose to be born again in order to find them.
To restore them to us.

The dreamtime ....

But once again, we lost our way and we died.
It is a never-ending story of mother and father
seeking daughter and son.
And daughter and son
seeking mother and father.
There are so many of us now.
Constantly reproducing ourselves
as mother, father, daughter, son.
We have been born so many times.
Lifetime after lifetime.
One lifetime, born as the Mother.
Another lifetime, born as the Father
Another lifetime,
born as the Daughter or the Son.
And each lifetime we are born with
a new name and a new body and a new face.
We no longer know who is who.
We are hopelessly lost.
Am I your father or your son?
Are you my mother or my daughter?
Or am I mother, father, daughter, son.
And am I seeking outside of myself
that which I am?

Who are you?

Your relationships are not what they appear to be.
Is your husband really your father or your son?
Is your wife really your mother or your daughter?
Do you dare to answer these questions honestly?
And who are you?
Are you mother, daughter, father, son?

He is not your son

He is not your son.
He is The Son.
She is not your daughter.
She is The Daughter.
He is not your father.
He is The Father.
She is not your mother.
She is The Mother.

There is only one son.

There is only one Mother.
There is only one Father.
There is only one Son.
There is only one Daughter.
Every birth of a male child
is an expression of the one Son.
Every birth of a female child
is an expression of the One Daughter.
Every mother is an expression of the One Mother.
Every Father is an expression of the One Father.

There is only One God

There is but One True God who is the source
of all creation both in Heaven and on Earth.
Everything in existence is an emanation
of the One True God.
Divine Mother is an emanation of the One True God.
Heavenly Father is an emanation
of the One True God.
Christ is an emanation of the One True God.
Magdalene is an emanation of the One True God.
This is the Divine Family of God.
Mother, Father, Daughter, Son.

All of humanity is an extension
of the Divine Family.

God is

God is the infinite source of all life.
God is the infinite source of all light.
God is the infinite source of all love.
God is the infinite source of all bliss.
God is the infinite source of all joy.
God is the infinite source.
God is.

I am the One

I am the One.
In the beginning, I am the One.
At the end, I am the One.
In between, I am the One.

Accepting change

Be comfortable with change.
Flow with change.
Everything around you is changing.
The only thing that is constant is change.
The more you accept change within your life
the more you will come to know yourself
as the one who never changes.

The eternal realm

In the eternal realm, there is no time
and so nothing changes.
Nothing is born and nothing dies.
Nothing grows old.

The river and the stream

The soul is like a river travelling through time.
It journeys across many lifetimes,
acquiring a sense of identity as it goes.
Each lifetime lived in physical form contributes
to the soul's sense of it's own identity in much the
same way that each significant event in your life
contributes to your sense of identity.
If in an earlier incarnation, you were aggressive,
controlling and selfish, without care or regard
for others, those negative human personality
traits and the karmic consequences of your
thoughts and deeds during that lifetime,
would have passed into the soul
at the time of your death.
This would have added to the soul's sense of
separation and its sense of unworthiness.
In subsequent incarnations, the soul will seek to
overcome those negative traits and will enter
into a life script which will give the soul
it's best opportunity to learn its lessons,
as well as to release and repay karmic debt.
Its purpose is to evolve
towards Oneness with God.
The soul is Eternal, but it exists within a realm
where to varying degrees it experiences
itself as separate from God.

The river and the stream ....

The more evolved the individual soul,
the less it feels separate.
The soul is like a river seeking
to cleanse itself of all its impurities.
Every now and then, it channels into a smaller
stream which separates from the river of the soul
and winds its way through just one lifetime.
This stream, journeying through one lifetime
is the personality which develops into the ego.
It is through the development of the ego
that the soul will eventually learn its lessons
and free itself from the illusion of separation.
It is only by journeying into separation,
that the illusion of separation can be overcome.
Hopefully, the soul's journey through this one
lifetime will result in the purification
and evolution of the soul.
When the body dies, the personality or ego
returns to the soul and is absorbed.
The stream disappears into the river.
The soul is deeply affected by the ego's return.
Its sense of its own identity is affected by
whatever is brought back by the ego.
Has the ego succeeded in its journey
upon behalf of the soul?

The river and the stream ....

Have the lessons been learned?
Is the soul purified by the return of the ego?
Or has the ego brought back
to the soul unresolved traumas,
repressed feelings, unfulfilled desires,
misunderstandings, bitterness, conflict,
isolation, fear and a sense of failure?
Has the ego managed to free itself from
Karmic debt? Or has it created even more
karmic consequences which will have to be
worked out in future incarnations?
Is the river cleaner or more
polluted by the return of the stream?
More likely than not, the soul will be required
to undergo further purification and so this
process of birth, death and rebirth will continue
until the soul is purified and is restored into
the experience of Oneness with God.
In other words, the river will continue
its journey through incarnation after
incarnation until it finally flows into
the Infinite and Eternal Ocean of Being.

Duality's classroom

At the level of ego,
we live our lives within duality.
Everything that we experience
within the world of time is experienced
within duality.
Everything we know is known
within the context of duality.
How can we know hot without cold?
How can we know long without short?
How can we know day without night?
How can we know acceptance without rejection?
How can we know joy without pain?
How can we know life without death?
How can we know Oneness without separation?
How can we know the presence of God
without knowing the absence of God?
Duality is our classroom and life is our teacher.

Which lessons did you come here to learn?
Your whole life will be a reflection
of these lessons.

Everything that occurs in your life
is an opportunity for learning.

The soul's lessons

If you reflect upon the key themes and events
in your life, particularly those which you would
label as negative, difficult or painful,
you will begin to identify some of the lessons
which you have come here to learn in this lifetime.
If rejection has been a major theme in your life,
then you must have come here to learn
about acceptance.
It is that simple.
In a previous incarnation,
you may have experienced a lot of hurt and anger
which arose around the issue of rejection.
At the soul level, you decided to incarnate again
in order to release the hurt and anger
and the feelings of rejection from the soul
as well as bring back to the soul the experience
of love and acceptance.
To incarnate into the realm of the ego
is the only way for the soul to purify itself
and learn its lessons.
It is only by entering into the separation
that the illusion of separation can be overcome.
The soul knows that all learning occurs
within duality.

The soul's lessons ....

It knows that in order to learn about acceptance,
it will have to go through the experience of
rejection and so, prior to your current incarnation,
the soul writes its script very carefully.
The script is cast with you in the starring role.
Your mother and your father
are key supporting players in your script.
You know that your prospective mother has
experienced a lot of rejection in her life.
You know that she is angry.
You know that she is afraid of intimacy.
You know that she is unlikely to be there for you,
because nobody has been there for her.
You know that your prospective father is
judgmental and critical. You know that he will have
high expectations of you and that he will not accept
you unless you meet those expectations.
You can see that these two people are perfect for
your script. They will provide you with ample
experience of rejection, which is the only way
you will be able to enter into the experience
of acceptance.
With your parents carefully selected,
you are conceived in your mother's womb.

The soul's lessons ....

You come into existence in physical form.
You have high hopes of learning
your soul's lesson in this lifetime.
The moment you are conceived however,
you forget who you are and why you are here.
You forget that you have written the script
in perfect detail. You forget what it is
that you have come here to learn.
All you know is that you are experiencing
a lot of rejection and you don't like it.
It is too painful.
You feel hurt and angry.
You are just a child.
You begin to reject the experiences of rejection
which you yourself have written into the script.
That which you reject always rises up
to claim you as its own.
As you repress the feelings of rejection, hurt
and anger, you find yourself locked into these
very feelings at an unconscious level.
You then live a life filled with rejection,
hurt and anger.
And then you die.

The soul's lessons ....

When you die, you are restored
to consciousness at the soul level.
You remember the lesson you were supposed to
learn. You remember the detailed script that you
wrote for yourself. You realize that you failed to
learn your lesson and so you begin preparations to
repeat the whole sorry episode.
Perhaps you have been repeating the same lesson
and the same story lifetime after lifetime.
A different name.
A different body.
Different players, different costumes
but the same script.
You would be wise to look very carefully
at the story of your life.
Examine the script closely.
What do the circumstances of your life
reveal to you.
What are you here to learn.
It is not too late.
Life is your teacher.
Learn your lessons now.

Life is a mirror.
It reflects back to you everything
you need to know.

Joy and pain

If you have come here to learn about and
experience joy, then you will have to create
a certain amount of pain in your life.
Joy and pain are dual aspects of each other.
They define each other.
You cannot know one without the other.
Pain is a messenger of God.
It is your teacher.
It has come into your life to teach you about joy.
It contains within it all the clues
that will reveal to you just how you manage
to keep joy out of your life.
If you avoid the pain, you will miss the lessons.
You do not have to linger in the pain.
All you have to do is accept and experience
the pain and it will reveal its secrets to you.
Then you will be released from the pain.
You will be released into joy.

Joy and pain ....

It is the same with anger and compassion,
sadness and happiness, fear and love,
control and freedom.
Whatever it is that you have come here to learn,
you will have to experience its dual nature.
Sadness is the doorway
through which you must pass
on the way to happiness.
Pain is the doorway to joy.
Death is the doorway to life.
And separation is the doorway to Oneness.
You cannot know one without the other.
It would be wise to relax
and embrace both sides of duality.
It will create balance in your life.
It will deliver you into the center.

Emotional pain

Emotional pain precedes physical pain.
If you feel and experience the emotional pain,
it will deliver its message to you.
It will reveal to you exactly what you need to know.
It will provide you with very appropriate clues
on the best way to respond to whatever
is happening in your life.
There will be no need for physical pain.
But if you ignore the emotional pain
and fail to respond appropriately,
then a certain level of dis-ease will gradually
manifest in your physical body.
This dis-ease will eventually produce physical pain.
Pain is persistent. It wants to deliver its message.

Other lessons to learn

You might be here to learn
about the true nature of love and freedom.
You might be here to awaken the qualities
of compassion and loving kindness within you.
You might be here to embrace true responsibility
and release your soul from the tendency towards
blame and guilt. You might be here to overcome the
idea imprinted into the soul from earlier
incarnations that you are a victim, so that you can
stop acting out the role of victim. You might be
here to discover how and why you lose your
sense of Self in others. You might be here to atone
for past actions or to heal past relationships.
There are many lessons we are here to learn
but all these lessons are intended to open
us up to a higher learning.
Eventually, we will have to learn
the art of living in balance within duality.
We will have to see through the veils of illusion.
We will have to come to the realization that the
world of the thinking mind is a world of illusion.
We will have to bring the ego to a place of
surrender as we awaken into the truth of Being.
We will have to awaken out of the past and
future into the reality of the present moment.
We will have to dissolve the illusion of separation
and return to Oneness with God.

The master lesson

There are many lessons to be learned
over many lifetimes.
Lessons about love, truth,
power, acceptance and compassion.
But the master lesson is the lesson of Oneness.
We are here to remember who we are.
We are here to awaken
out of the illusion of separation.
We are here to know and experience
ourselves as One with God.
We are here to awaken fully
into the present moment which is the key
to awakening and the doorway to God.
We must discover how we are creating
the illusion of separation in our lives.
How do we keep ourselves imprisoned
within the world of the thinking mind?
What is it that separates us from God?
Attachment to the past separates us from God.
Desire, which involves us in the future, separates us
from God. Holding onto resentment or past hurt
separates us from God. Judgment, blame and guilt
separate us from God. Looking outside of ourselves
for love and acceptance separates us from God.
Fear separates us from God.
Patterns of control separate us from God.

The master lesson ....

Patterns of emotional reaction
separate us from God.
Our thoughts, beliefs and opinions
separate us from God.
Even our belief in God separates us from God.
Anything which takes us out of the present
moment into the world of the thinking mind
separates us from God.
The present moment is the doorway to God.
It is the doorway to the Eternal.
If you can master the art of being fully present,
then you have learned the master lesson.
You will have liberated yourself
from the prison of the thinking mind.
You will have overcome the illusion of separation.
You will be restored to Oneness.
It is a lesson that will be delivered to your soul,
not at the time of your death, but immediately.
The soul will be transformed.
The soul will be healed.
The soul will be restored to Oneness.
To learn the master lesson
is to be the Savior of your soul.
Through your efforts,
your soul will be delivered into
the conscious experience of immortality.

From duality to Oneness

You cannot arrive at Oneness
by denying the negative aspects
of duality and focusing on the positive.
You awaken into Oneness by bringing
the positive and negative aspects of duality
into balance within you.
This is accomplished by transcending
judgment and by being willing to experience
both the positive and the negative aspects
of duality within you.
The positive and the negative
are equal in the context of Oneness.
Both the positive and the negative
are essential in a dual existence.
The positive and the negative define each other.
One cannot be known without the other.
When you bring duality into balance in this way,
you reveal the Oneness that exists at the
very heart and essence of everything.

All that exists is You

At the very deepest level,
there is no ego,
there is no soul,
there is no spirit.
There is no journey.
There is no separation.
There are no other realms.
Everything has come together as One.
All that exists is You.
Present.
Complete.
Whole.
Fully immersed in the mystery
of this moment.

When I am fully present,
my past is not here to define me.

Death is the doorway to life

Death is the doorway to life.
By death, I do not mean
the death of the physical body.
To die means to die to the past.
It means to surrender all attachment to the past.
It means letting go of the past completely.
Life exists only in the present moment.
Unless you die to the past,
you cannot know the present.
Unless you know the present,
you cannot know life.
When the time comes for your physical body
to die, then the same principles apply.
Just die to the past.
Don't hold onto anything from the past.
Not even your body.
It has served you well.
Now let it go.

The awakened state

Whenever you feel caught up in the world
of experience and you have lost your sense
of Presence, ask yourself the following question.
"Who is experiencing?"
Experiences are many,
but the experiencer is One.
To know yourself as the One at the center
of all experience is to know the awakened state.

Beyond all experience
is the One who is experiencing.
Beyond all change is the One who never changes.

The journey goes on forever.
Just be here now.

I am

I am God the Mother.
I am God the Father.
I am Christ.
I am Magdalene.
I am.

I am

I am Adam, the first man.
I am the beast before Adam.
I am the trees and the flowers.
I am the animals and the insects.
I am the snake and the spider.
I am the rocks and the mountains.
I am the ocean and the sand.
I am the birds and the sky.
I am all that is.
I am.

I am Buddha, the pure mind of God.
I am Jesus, the pure heart of God.
I am Lao Tzu, the way of God in the world.

I am the destroyer

I am the destroyer.
I have come to destroy
the old to make way for the new.
But what is being destroyed?
The false is being destroyed.
Belief in illusion is being destroyed.
The power of belief is being destroyed.
Control over others is being destroyed.
Dishonesty is being destroyed.
Abuse of our environment and abuse of others
is being destroyed.
False Gods and false paths to God are being
destroyed. Relationships based on
fear and control are being destroyed.
Blind obedience to authority is being destroyed.
Injustice, inequity and intolerance are being
destroyed. Greed is being destroyed.
Judgment is being destroyed.
Attachment to the past is being destroyed.
The illusion of separation from God
is being destroyed.
The world we have known and lived in for many
lifetimes is slowly being taken away from us.
It is creating a great deal of insecurity.
It is creating fear at many levels.
The old is breaking down
but the new is not yet here.

I am the destroyer ....

Destruction can be catastrophic
or it can be a loving and gentle process.
It depends on how much we resist.
The more we resist, the more difficult
and traumatic is the destruction.
Destruction of the old is essential
in giving birth to the new.
This is a fundamental principle of consciousness.
It is a fundamental principle of existence.
As you awaken and open to the presence of God
and as you surrender your attachment to the past,
fear and the insecurity begin to diminish.
Embrace what is unfolding
through the present moment.
Be brave. Be strong.
Ask for God's guidance.
There is a new world dawning.
Your life and your experience over many
lifetimes has been but a preparation
for the dawning of the new world.
I speak of the coming of Heaven to Earth.
You have chosen to live during this time.
Recognize your true purpose in being here.
Complete your soul's journey in this lifetime.
You are the bridge between Heaven and Earth.
It is in you that God will be restored to the One.
It is in you that God's original vision will be realized.

Waiting for the Messiah

The Jews could not accept Jesus when he appeared
as the Messiah. They had been waiting for the
Messiah for centuries.
They had access to the higher levels
through their mystical traditions.
They knew that he would
appear from the higher realms.
They expected him to bring forth
a period of creation,
a period of healing and love.
At first he fulfilled their expectations.
He seemed to be the Messiah.
But then the message of Jesus changed.
He began to speak of division and destruction.
He said that he had come to set brother against
brother and father against son.
The people could not understand
what he was talking about.
He spoke in parables that were not easily
understood. They are still not easily understood.
He opposed Jewish hypocrisy whenever
and wherever he encountered it.
His message could be seen as taking power and
authority away from the rabbis. He spoke of a
personal and private relationship with God.
He described himself as One with God,
which was considered blasphemous.

Waiting for the Messiah ....

And so the majority of Jews rejected Jesus as the
Messiah. They are still waiting for the Messiah.
Just as the Christians are waiting for
the second coming of Christ.
But if Christ were to come again,
the Christians would reject him for exactly
the same reasons that the Jews rejected him
the first time. They would not be able
to accept his simple message.
It would be too threatening for them.
It would not correspond
to their existing understanding.
But what is the point of a Messiah who brings
to you a message which you already know?
If there is to be a second coming of Christ,
it will have to be Jesus.
The Christians will not accept a second coming
of Christ who is not Jesus.
He would have to look exactly like the pictures
of Jesus hung on their walls and nailed onto their
wooden crosses.
He would have to perform miracles to prove
to them that he is the Christ come again.
If Christ were to come again, he would oppose
Christian hypocrisy whenever and wherever he
encountered it. It would not be a very comfortable
experience for the Christians.

Waiting for the Messiah ....

His message would be very threatening
to the power and authority of the popes
and the archbishops.
He would immediately declare that the priest
is not your father and that the minister
is not God's representative.
He would speak of a personal and private
relationship you must have with God.
He would tell you that no one should
stand between you and God.
Not even him.
He would share with you the laws of God.
He would show you how to be
in right relationship with God.
He would show you how to escape
the tyranny and bondage of the mind.
He would remind you that if you are to know
God in your life, then you must first embrace
true responsibility.
He would reveal to you that the test that you must
pass is the test of judgment. You must transcend
all judgment in your life before you can know God.
He would show you the way.
But you would have to walk the path alone.
He will not save you.
You will have to save yourself.

The true mission of Christ

Christ's mission on Earth began
with the birth of Jesus.
But it did not end with his death.
It will not be completed
until the Second Coming of Christ.
It is a mission which has been unfolding
for almost two thousand years.
It cannot be understood
from any one point in time.
It must be viewed from a higher
and broader perspective.
It must be viewed from the eternal realm.
You will have to step outside of time
if you really want to understand
the true mission of Christ.

Christ

Christ is a state of consciousness.
In physical form, he is Awakened Man.
He is the Healer.
He will make you whole.
Magdalene is a state of consciousness.
In physical form, she is Awakened Woman.
She is the nurturer.
She will tend to you.

Magdalene

Magdalene.
She is the daughter of the Earth.
She is her Mother's child.
She is the embodiment of tender love.
She is the Nurturer.
She is Nature itself.
She is the bestower of life.
She is tenderness.
She tends to the fallen male
for she knows that he is her fallen Father
and he is her fallen Son.
What else can she do but love him
and tend to him.
And wait until he recognizes her
and remembers
who he is.

Christ consciousness

Christ is a state of consciousness
which arises when man and God
meet and become One.
Jesus the man became Jesus the Christ
in those moments of perfect Oneness with God.

The truth about Jesus

Christians believe that Jesus surrendered
to the death of his physical body
and died for their sins.
But the crucifixion of Jesus
was not about his physical death.
He was not afraid of dying.
He was way beyond identification
with his physical body.
It was not fear of death that caused
him to cry out in despair,
"Hast Thou forsaken me?"
He could feel himself falling in consciousness.
He could feel his connection with God slipping
away. He could feel himself falling to the level of
consciousness of those he had come to save.
The Christ in Jesus was fading.
He was slipping away from God.
He was dying as the Christ.
All the pain and fear and suffering
of the world flooded into him.
And then he died.
This innocent messenger of God
had been rejected, tortured and killed
in the severest of ways.
But the death of his physical body and the pain
and suffering he endured on the cross
was not the true sacrifice.

The truth about Jesus ....

He was about to become the Lamb of God
in a way that few people could possibly realize.
He was about to embark
upon a journey though time.
It was a journey through the realm
of the human mind and ego.
It was a journey into separation and darkness.
It was intended by God that he would explore
and experience the human heart and mind in an
endeavor to find the keys to love and liberation.
If he could find his way through,
then the Way would be revealed for others.
This involved incarnating lifetime after lifetime
in the same way and in the same circumstances
that a less evolved soul would incarnate.
It also involved entering into and experiencing
the darker side of human nature, in an effort
to understand why man would inflict
such suffering upon his brothers and sisters.
Sometimes he would incarnate as the tortured
and the innocent. At other times, he would
incarnate as the torturer and the guilty.
Sometimes he would suffer at the hands
of the cruel and the loveless. At other times
he would be the one inflicting the suffering.

The truth about Jesus ....

Sometimes he incarnated as a teacher of truth.
At other times, he incarnated as a cruel and
controlling leader who exploited his people
or a ruthless general in the army
who would triumph from the horror of war.
Sometimes he would incarnate as an animal
to experience the suffering of animals.
Or an orphan, to experience the plight
of lost children.
By playing out all the roles involved in human
suffering, he was able to gain invaluable insight
into the nature of the mind and the reasons why
humanity had become so lost in the realm of the ego.
What had gone wrong?
Why was it so difficult for human Beings to awaken
into love and the truth of life? Why was it so difficult
for human Beings to escape the tyranny and bondage
of the human mind? Why had the ego become so
powerful? Why had it become so difficult to
overcome the experience of separation and return to
Oneness with God?
In a sense, the one who had been Jesus took on the
karma of others, lifetime after lifetime and he lived
out the consequences of that karma until all the
varieties of human experience were known to him.

The truth about Jesus ....

In this way, it can be said that Jesus
died for the sins of others.
His journey would not be over until he had
unraveled the mystery of the human dilemma.
With very little break between lifetimes,
he has continued on his way,
lost like everyone else in the maze
of the human mind, unable to find his way
back to God.
It was a difficult journey, leading him
further and further into the darkness.
Each time he incarnated, he had no conscious
awareness that he had once been Jesus.
He suffered along with every one else,
not knowing the truth of his own identity.
With each successive incarnation,
it was becoming more difficult for him to awaken.
In this current incarnation, however,
he has found the way through.
The keys to liberation have been
revealed to him.
His ordeal on the cross is over.
He has undergone a resurrection,
two thousand years after his fall on the cross.
He has remembered who he is.
He is restored to truth, love and Oneness.
He is restored to God.

The fallen Christ is within you
The time of the Resurrection is Now

The fall of Jesus was an event that would have
a profound impact upon the future awakening
of human consciousness.
In that moment of the fall on the cross,
the consciousness of Jesus Christ
became a seed of Christ consciousness,
planted by God within the mind of man.
The consciousness of the Christ in Jesus had
been sacrificed into the collective human mind.
Over the past two thousand years, that seed
of Christ consciousness has been slowly
and gradually taking root, finding fertile soil
within individuals who are spiritually mature
enough to receive it and nurture it into the full
flowering of Christ consciousness within them.
As the seed of Christ consciousness awakens fully
within an individual, he or she will begin to
experience Oneness with God in much the
same way that Jesus did during his lifetime.
This is what is meant by Christ consciousness.
To awaken into Christ consciousness is to know
yourself as One with God. To awaken into Christ
consciousness is to awaken into the Eternal
dimension of life.

The resurrection of Christ

I have been asked if the resurrection of Christ
actually occurred three days after his death as
revealed in the New Testament.
My answer is simply this.
It did occur but it was an event that occurred at
the spiritual level and not the physical level.
It was the spiritual body of Jesus and not the
physical body that the disciples saw.
Jesus appeared to his disciples as a shimmering
body of light, although he may have at times
appeared almost physical in form.
The spiritual dimension of Jesus has existed within
the spiritual realm ever since the crucifixion.
However, at another level of consciousness,
the one who had been Jesus embarked upon a
journey into separation and darkness.
It was as if a split had occurred within the
consciousness of Jesus at the time of the crucifixion.
In that moment of death on the cross, a significant
part of the consciousness of Jesus split off and
experienced the fall. It was a terrifying fall,
which led into a painful and difficult journey
through the realm of the ego and that
dimension of the soul, which is engaged in
an endless cycle of birth, death and rebirth.

The resurrection of Christ ....

It was a journey into darkness,
which would last for almost two thousand years.
It was a journey directed by God in every detail.
The beloved Son of God would become
the Lamb of God in an effort to find
the keys to love and liberation.
When the one who had been Jesus
was restored to God in this lifetime,
it signaled the Second Coming of Christ.
It opened a door within human consciousness,
which revealed the Way out of separation
into Oneness. The ordeal of Christ on the cross
is over. The split in the consciousness
of Jesus has been healed.
The second coming of Christ is now unfolding
within the collective levels of human consciousness.
Many are beginning to awaken.
Many are experiencing Oneness with God.
To know yourself as One with God is to be
restored into the consciousness of Christ.
To know yourself as One with God
is to be Christ resurrected.

The Journey of Jesus

Before this journey started, I was with God.
It was wonderful.
I was in the realm of Eternal Oneness.
It was so rich and full and abundant.
It truly was Paradise. I was blissfully unaware
that there were other realms of the Kingdom.
One day, one of God's servants came up to me
and took my hand. "Come with me," he said.
"I want to show you something."
He took me to an opening which was covered
by a curtain. As he drew the curtain back,
I was able to see through time and space into
another dimension of existence. I was fascinated.
There were Beings who looked similar to me living
out their lives in a strange yet familiar place.
It was hot and dry and the land was parched.
The people seemed to be suffering.
They were in great pain.
Their world was a world of darkness without love.
It was a world without God.
It was a world without truth.
It was a world of fear and separation.
The whole point of their existence
seemed to be to gain control.
They seemed intent on dominating each other.

The Journey of Jesus ....

The men would dominate the women.
The strong would dominate the weak.
The many would dominate the few.
The rich would dominate the poor.
They were hopelessly lost.
They longed for love but they lived in fear.
They even feared God.
Their God was a God of judgment,
a God of vengeance.
"How strange!" I thought to myself.
It seemed so removed and distant
from my heavenly abode.
I watched on in fascination.
I saw a woman give birth to a son.
I watched as he grew into an adult.
He married and had many children.
He worked hard.
He attained a certain measure of success
and power, which seemed in some way to
be a measure of his worth. He accumulated
considerable wealth and then he died.
He had no idea who he really was
or what was his true purpose.
Suddenly, I saw the same man born again
but this time to a different mother.

The Journey of Jesus ....

He had a different name and a different body
but it was the same man. I could see clearly that
he was about to repeat his whole life again.
"I have seen enough," I said to the guide.
The guide closed the curtain carefully.
"Who are these people?" I asked.
"They are the lost souls," replied the guide.
"Where are they lost?" I asked.
"They are lost somewhere in time.
They are lost in a world of illusion.
They are lost in a world of separation.
They are lost in a world which they have created
in their own minds and now they cannot find
their way out. It is not a real world but they have
come to believe that it is real.
They live in a world of belief.
As long as they continue to believe in their
world and their ideas and their opinions,
they will never find their way home."
"Where is their home?" I asked.
"Their home is here," answered the guide.
"They are one of us."
My heart filled with compassion.
"Why did they leave?" I asked,
with some feeling of concern.

The Journey of Jesus ....

"They left in loving and devoted service to God!"
replied the guide. "But they became lost."
"Hasn't anyone tried to help them?" I asked.
"Many have tried," answered the guide.
"But they too have become lost. They too have
become caught up in the world of illusion.
Very few have found the way back.
And so now, no one will even try."
"I will go," I said.
"There must be some way to assist these people."
"No!" said the guide.
"We could not bear to lose you!"
"I will do my Father's work," I said
and before the guide could stop me,
I had plunged through the opening
and found myself falling into endless darkness.
I was disappearing into nothing.
"This is just the beginning," I said to myself
as I relaxed. "I trust in God, who is my Father
and I am sure that He will light my way."
I opened my eyes. It was difficult to see at first.
I felt quite helpless. I was in a baby's body.
But I knew who I was and I knew
why I had come here.

The Journey of Jesus ....

I felt so full and clear and alive.
I was still in Paradise but it felt different.
I had been in a baby's body before,
but it was not real. The world I had come from had
no physical form. I had created my body with my
mind. I had created the physical world I lived in
with my mind. But the body I was in now
was real and it felt exquisite.
"This is my beloved Son," I heard my mother say.
She drew me to her breast and I was flooded
with a love which I had never experienced before.
It was the love of my Mother and I found myself
melting into her. I was merging into her. I was
becoming one with her. She was so loving
and pure and innocent.
As I grew older, I was taught the ways of the world
which I now lived in. Gradually, I forgot who I was
and where I had come from. The memory of why I
had come to this world had completely faded.
I learned a trade and began work as a carpenter.
I lived my life fully, but I could not escape
the feeling that something was missing.
Something was wrong.
More and more I was becoming solitary.
I felt that I was an outsider.
I did not fit into this world.

The Journey of Jesus ....

All around me people were suffering.
People were in pain.
They turned to God and the Holy Scriptures,
but it did not seem to help them.
They prayed for the Messiah.
They prayed for deliverance.
But their prayers went unanswered.
One day I encountered a man by the river Jordan.
He spoke in a way that excited me.
Something deep within me was stirred.
He was baptizing people in the water.
He held their heads under the water for a
long time, almost to the point where they
could die for lack of breath.
As soon as they struggled, he would release
them and they came out of the water
gasping for breath and for life.
I could not really see the point to it, but
I stepped forward and I too was immersed
in the water.
I had decided not to struggle.
I trusted that this man would not let me die.
I was held under the water for a long time.
It seemed like forever.

The Journey of Jesus ....

I wanted to struggle but then I felt myself surrender.
"If I am to die then so be it," I said to myself.
I felt myself passing into endless darkness.
I felt myself disappearing into nothing.
I surrendered completely.
At last my head was lifted out of the water.
The man smiled at me.
"I love you," he said.
We embraced and then I left.
I knew I had to walk alone into the desert.
Something new and beautiful had awakened
within me. Somehow, I had been called by God.
I could feel the presence of God unfolding
within me but first, I knew I had to purify myself.
I set off into the desert without food and only a
little water. The days were long and extremely hot.
The evenings were cold and lonely. In all this time,
I did not sleep. My throat was parched and dry.
I was extremely tired and yet I felt completely
awake. I had lost track of the days and nights.
Then, one late afternoon as the sun was setting,
I had a vision. Satan appeared before me in the
desert. He had come to tempt me.
He had come to claim me as his own.

The Journey of Jesus ....

"Why do you go hungry?" asked Satan.
"If God is with you, then just turn these stones
into bread. Feed yourself."
"Bread can fill my body," I answered.
"But only God can fill my life. I will not
use the power of God to feed myself."
"Prove to me who you are!" said Satan.
"Cast yourself from the highest temple.
If God is truly with you, you will not be harmed."
"I will not put God to the test," I replied.
"God does not have to prove himself to you."
"I offer you power and glory and the riches of all
the kingdoms if you will but serve me," said Satan.
"I serve only God," I answered and with that Satan
was gone. My encounter with Satan was extremely
useful. I was purified of any unconscious or hidden
desires. It had become clear that I would not misuse
the power of God in any way and that I would not
succumb to the desire for personal power and
recognition. As soon as Satan was sure that
I was a true Servant of God, I was released
from further temptation.

The Journey of Jesus ....

After my sojourn in the desert,
the presence of God filled me completely.
I gathered together a small number of people
and we began roaming the countryside.
I shared my simple message
with all those who would hear.
"The Promised Land which you seek is within you.
It cannot be found outside of you."
For me, it was no longer the Promised Land
for I was in the Kingdom of Heaven.
I was in the Kingdom of my Father.
"The Kingdom of Heaven is within," I said.
"The time of deliverance is now."
I shared the truth and the way with
all who would listen.
"Only if you are in right relationship with God
will the Sacred Covenant be fulfilled. Only then
will you be delivered unto the Promised Land."
But very few could hear me. For the truth has no
power to penetrate into the world of belief.
Belief must dissolve of its own accord
before the truth can enter.
I felt the light of God shining like a rising sun
within me. God filled me completely.
People were made whole in my presence.
I traveled the countryside speaking and sharing
the words as they arose within me.

The Journey of Jesus ....

Many wanted to be healed but very few
could hear my simple message.
Gradually, the words began to change.
I found myself speaking of division and destruction.
It was not what the Rabbis had expected of the
Messiah. They could not accept my teachings.
They were turning against me. I had been told
by the voice of God that I would be put to death.
I was told that I would be betrayed.
I agreed to this and prepared those who were
closest to me for this event. We shared dinner
together and then the authorities came for me.
I was forced to carry a heavy wooden cross
to my place of execution. I did not understand
why this had to happen but I trusted.
Eventually we arrived and I was nailed
to the cross. The cross was raised upright
and my crucifixion began. Blood flowed freely
from where the nails had pierced my body.
I looked out and saw the faces
of those who had loved me.
My mother was there. She was weeping.
Magdalene was there.
I saw a number of familiar faces in the crowd.
But most were just onlookers.

The Journey of Jesus ....

I experienced no pain.
I was filled with the light and presence of God.
Never before had I felt so at one with my Father.
It was as if I was already at home even though
my body was firmly nailed to the cross.
Suddenly the light began to fade.
I could feel the presence of God leaving me.
The physical pain flooded in.
I was overwhelmed with despair and confusion.
What had I done wrong?
Had I failed God in some way?
Had I loved these people too much?
Had I told them more than I should have?
Had I misled them in some way?
All these questions arose in an instant.
I looked out and all I could see was despair.
I looked down and unimaginable terror arose
within me. For the very Earth itself had opened up
beneath me. The past, like a thousand snakes
in a bottomless pit rose up to swallow me.
I was about to fall.
To the very beginning of time.
I was filled with the suffering of ages past.
"Hast Thou forsaken me?" I cried.

The Journey of Jesus ....

And then I heard these words.
"The first shall be last and the last shall be first
and they shall be a single One."
It was the voice of God.
I relaxed and let go of the fear.
"Thy will be done," I said silently to my beloved
Father. I surrendered to the Fall.
And then I died.
The fall on the cross, which had lasted
only a few minutes was soon to unfold through
many levels and dimensions and would
continue for almost two thousand years.
I have lived many lifetimes since then.
I have been through the full range of human
experience during these last two thousand years.
I have experienced all the human emotions.
I have experienced all the forms of suffering.
I have experienced isolation and despair.
I have experienced the pain of separation from God
which is the true source of all pain and suffering.
I have encountered all the forms of evil known to
man. I have experienced judgment over and over
again. I have experienced the deepest feelings
of guilt and shame.

The Journey of Jesus ....

It seemed as though I was taking all the pain and
suffering of the world upon my own shoulders.
The realm of the human mind is like an endless
labyrinth. It is an intricate web of illusion
from which there is no escape.
I could not find the way out, no matter how
hard I tried. I studied all the religious teachings.
I followed all the spiritual paths.
But still I could not find the way out.
I had no idea who I had been
or why I had come here.
I have carried the memory of my earlier life
within me at the deepest and most hidden level
for almost two thousand years and until now,
I have been unable to restore that memory
into my consciousness.
It was too frightening for me to accept.
I had taken on the suffering of the whole world.
The pain and fear and guilt of every human being
was placed upon my shoulders.
The cross was now weighed down
with the suffering of all humanity.
And I accepted this burden willingly,
believing in some way that I had failed God.

The Journey of Jesus ....

I had no way of knowing that in this lifetime
I would be restored to God. I had no way of
knowing that my pain and suffering would be
turned so completely into love and compassion.
I had no way of knowing that my feelings of
isolation and separation would be turned so
completely into Oneness and perfect union.
I had no way of knowing that everything
which had unfolded over the past two thousand
years had unfolded perfectly according
to the will of God.
I had no way of knowing that the time
of the Resurrection is now.
In this lifetime, all has been revealed.
The Savior has been saved.
The fallen Jesus is resurrected.
I came as the Son of God.
But now I come as the Son of Man.
For I AM the Second Coming of Christ.
And my message has not changed.
That which you seek is within you.
As Jesus, I had awakened as the Christ.
Christ is the consciousness that exists when
man and God meet and become One.

The Journey of Jesus ....

The Jesus in me had ascended from man.
The Christ in me had descended from God.
At my death on the cross, I had fallen and in falling,
I had taken Christ with me into the mind of man.
I believed at the time that I had failed God
but I know now that this was not so. For I am
much loved by God for my surrender to the fall.
In truth, I am the Lamb of God but I knew it not.
For it was God's intention that I would fall.
It was the only way for God to enter into the mind
of man. How could I have known that God
would enter as the fallen Christ.
Jesus no longer exists.
I am someone else now.
I have a new body and a new name.
The memory of Jesus on the cross
has been brought to consciousness and released.
And so the journey of Jesus is over.
But the resurrection of Christ has only just begun.
For the fallen Christ is within each one of you.
And the time of the Resurrection is now.
If the resurrection can occur within one,
then it can occur within all.
For my story is your story.
I have come to show you the way,
for it is time to come home.

I am the way, the truth and the life

"I am the way, the truth and the life."
These words in the New Testament
are attributed to Jesus.
Never before in the history of mankind
has one sentence led humanity so far astray.
The whole of Christianity has been
misdirected by these words.
These few words have led Christians to believe
that they must go through Jesus to God.
They believed that Jesus was saying
that he was the way, the truth and the life.
That only through him can you
enter the Kingdom of God.
If Jesus really did utter these words,
then he made a terrible mistake.
For he left out one very important word from
that sentence which is crucial to
the true message of Christ.
It is a simple word with only two letters.
It is the word "IS."
If you insert the word "IS" into the sentence,
then it will read,
"I am IS the way, the truth and the life."
Just one simple word with two letters and the
whole of Christianity can be brought back on track.

I am the way, the truth and the life ....

My deepest conviction is that the mistake
was not made by Jesus but that it occurred
during the reporting of his words or the translation
of his words after his death.
For Jesus truly had awakened
to Christ Consciousness.
He had awakened to the consciousness of I AM.
He had awakened to Being.
He had awakened into the Eternal Now.
He had come to the center.
He had experienced himself as One with God.
He would have known that I AM is the way.
He would have known that for him, I AM is
within him. But for you, I AM is within you.
Jesus would never have intended to stand between
you and God. His whole message was contradictory
to that. He was so clear. The Kingdom of God is
within. It is within you. It is within me.
Jesus is gone. He is no longer in physical form.
He has done his part.
Now it is up to me.
Now it is up to you.
Awaken into the truth of life.
Awaken into Oneness with God.
Discover who you are.
Complete your soul's journey in this lifetime.

I celebrate the I AM that you are.

The I AM Presence

Whenever you read the words of Jesus
in the New Testament, ask yourself,
"Is this Jesus the man speaking or is it
the I AM Presence speaking from within him?"
It will help you to understand the true
meaning of the words of Christ.

The life of Jesus

The life of Jesus is a living demonstration
of right relationship with God.
The actual events that occurred during the life of
Jesus show us as much about right relationship with
God as do his words.
The most profound aspects of his relationship
with God were his devotional love for God, a sense
of Oneness with God, and a deep recognition and
acknowledgment that God was the true source of
power in his life. The life of Jesus demonstrates
total surrender to the will of God.

When God knocks

Jesus said,
"Knock and the door shall be opened."
I say,
stop knocking.
Be still.
Be silent.
Be very alert.
Be very present.
For it is God who will knock.
And when God knocks,
open the door.
Do not hesitate.
Let God in.

Asking God

Jesus said, "Ask and Ye shall receive."
But you have to know how to ask.
Ask into the silence.
Ask with your body and your feelings.
Ask with your passion and your fury.
Ask with your love and your deepest longing.
Ask with your spirit and your soul.
Be honest with God.
Be authentic with God.
Be present with God.
This is true prayer.
And you do not know when God will respond.
You do not know how God will respond.
It is enough to know that God's response
is always perfect.

Knocking on God's door

Jesus said "Knock and the door shall be opened."
But you have to know how to knock.
The more silent your knock,
the louder it will be heard in Heaven.

Only one vine

Judaism, Christianity and Islam
are one vine planted by God.
Together they make up the whole.
Alone they are separate and incomplete.
As they exist now, they are condemned
to live in fear, conflict and struggle.
Each has the door closed on the other.
The doors will have to be opened.
There will have to be a coming
together of these three religions.
There will have to be a meeting in the middle.
Each needs the other to complete it
and make it whole.

Judaism, Christianity and Islam

Judaism has the goal.
It is the coming together of man and God.
The coming together of the above and the below.
The symbol of the Star of David
is a representation of this goal.
Jesus was a messenger of the Way.
The cross is a symbol which represents the Way,
although the true cross has the horizontal bar
at the very center of the vertical line of the cross.
It represents the transcendence of duality.
Mohammed was a Prophet whose role
was to reveal to us how we are meant
to live once we have found the Way
and arrived at the goal.
We are to live surrendered to the will of God.
The crescent moon is a symbol that reflects
our relationship to the whole.
Just to contemplate the relationship between
the partial crescent moon and the full moon
is deeply revealing of the true nature
of our existence and our relationship with God.

The Jews

The Jews have externalized the Promised Land.
They fight for the right to occupy Israel
and the Holy City of Jerusalem.
But the true Israel is within.
It is the inner realm of Being.
It is the realm of the One.
To experience the Promised Land within
is a blessing beyond words.
It is an experience of Heaven on Earth.
But to become permanently established in the
Promised Land is to find the inner Jerusalem.
Only then may you declare,
"I am Jacob become Israel."
This is why Jesus was so insistent
that the Kingdom is within.

To every Jew

It is time to fulfill your sacred Covenant with God.
Find your way into right relationship with God.
Find your way into true prayer.
Find your way into the present moment
which is the doorway to God.
Honor God above all.
Do not confuse ritual with Law.
The Promised Land is within.
The time of deliverance is now.

Do not be a Christian.
Be a Christ.
Do not be a Buddhist.
Be a Buddha.

There are many paths to God and the Truth,
but hidden within each one of these paths
is the One True Path.

A prayer before meditation

Know that God exists at the very heart
of silence within you.
When you pray to God, address your
prayers into the silence and make sure that
any response from God arises out of the silence.
Begin by expressing your love for God.
When you express your love for God,
it deepens you into Oneness.
It opens you into the Sacred and the Divine.
This is how I express my love for God.
"Beloved God, the Creator of everything.
Beloved God, the Creator and the Creation.
Beloved God, the One True God,
I am that I am.
Beloved God, the source of all light,
the source of all love,
the source of all power,
the source of all truth.
Beloved God,
I love You with all my heart.
I love You with all my soul.
I love You with all my body.
I love You with all my mind.
I love You with all my Being.

A prayer before meditation ....

Beloved God,
I offer myself to You in eternal love and devotion.
I offer myself to You in eternal gratitude.
I offer myself to You in eternal service.
I am Yours. Do with me as You will."
Be creative.
Find your own way to express your love for God.
This kind of expression opens up your heart.
It opens you into love.
At this point, pause and feel into the love.
Feel into the deep inner peace.
Relax into silence.
To be in a state of silent Presence
is to be in a state of true prayer.
Remain silent and fully present for
as long as you wish.
After some time, you may want to
express your gratitude towards God.
Be generous in your expression of gratitude.
God responds to gratitude more than anything else.
Thank God for everything that God has created.
Thank God for the gift of life
that you have been given.
Thank God for the lessons that you are here to
learn and tell God that you are ready to learn them.

A prayer before meditation …

If you are struggling to remain present and
loving in your life, then pray for healing.
Ask to be healed of any wound
from the past, which keeps you bound
within the illusion of separation.
Tell God that you want to awaken fully into love.
Ask to be cleared of any energy that is not love.
Ask to be filled with God's Light.
Ask to be filled with God's Love
and God's Perfect Presence.
Ask to be brought to a place
of perfect balance within you.
Ask to deepen into Oneness with God.
If you want, you can converse with God.
Just speak honestly and authentically into the silence.
Give God plenty of time to answer and be sure
that the answer arises out of the silence
and not from some part of your thinking mind.
The answer might come in the form of words.
It might come in the form of a visual image.
It might come as a feeling of love or peace or bliss.
Or the answer might come in the form of perfect
silence. As you deepen into the silence,
you deepen into Oneness.
You deepen into love.

Divine paradox

Whenever I speak about praying to God
or loving God, I am entering into a seemingly
impossible paradox.
If I am One with God, then how can
I pray to God? How can I love God?
To pray to God or love God implies two of us.
Me and God.
It takes me into duality.
It can so easily reinforce the notion
of separation from God.
How am I to live with this paradox?
The answer is subtle.
If I am always in a state of Oneness, then
there is no need for prayer or expression of love.
My whole life is a prayer and I am love.
I am a living expression of God.
I am God.
But if I find myself at times living in Oneness
and at other times living in the world of experience
within time and duality, then there is a place
for prayer and expression of love for God.

Divine paradox ....

Prayer can help to return me
into the experience of Oneness.
It can open me into a fuller experience of Love.
However, I must be careful not to externalize God
in my prayers. I do not want to reinforce
the illusion of separation when I pray,
which is what is happening in most of the
churches, temples and mosques
around the world.
I must always know that God is within
and that in truth, I am One with God.
I must always move from prayer
or expression of love into a deep and
expansive state of silence.
It is in the silence and the presence
that I enter into Communion with God.
It is in silence that I am One with God.
In the Oneness, I am and God is.
Separation dissolves.
All that remains is Eternal Presence.
Eternal is-ness.

A small degree of separation

I often speak of awakening fully into Oneness,
but why not allow the smallest degree
of separation to remain.
Just enough to allow you to express
your love and gratitude towards God.
You can move easily from Oneness
into the smallest degree of separation.
It is no more difficult than breathing.
Just do not go too far.
You might get caught in the mind.

Loving God

Some people find it difficult
to express their love for God.
In fact, they are angry with God.
They hate God.
They blame God for pain they have experienced.
They blame God for their suffering or the suffering
of their loved ones. How could a loving God
have allowed such suffering.
And so they have turned away from God.
They have closed off that part of their hearts
that was involved in loving God.
This is usually experienced at an unconscious
level and often originates in some distant past life.
It has taken them further into the illusion of
separation. It has taken them further
into the heart of darkness.
Their relationship with God has been damaged
and needs to be healed.
These wounds and feelings must be brought to
consciousness. They must be owned and
acknowledged. The feelings of hatred and
rage towards God must be expressed
and confessed.
God will not judge you or reject you.
God will love you for it.
It will return you to your love for God.
It will heal your heart.

Communion with God

Prayer, meditation, chanting, singing,
dancing and drumming are all wonderful ways
to free yourself from the limited world of the mind
and enter into a silent and dynamic communion
with God. Be creative. Find your own way
of relating to God.

The ego's surrender

If you are to know the truth,
the ego within you
will have to gradually surrender.
It must relax and let go.
It must let go of the need to be in control.
It must let go of the need to understand.
It must recognize that its world is not real.
It must accept that it is separate and that
it cannot overcome the separation.
It must surrender all judgment
including judgment of itself.
All it can do is relax and release you
into the truth and reality
of the present moment.

Trust and surrender

We can never know the whole picture.
It would be much wiser
to relax,
trust
and surrender
to the divine plan
as it unfolds within us.

The ego does not want you to wake up

The ego does not want you to wake up.
It will pretend that it wants you to wake up.
It will have you reading every spiritual book
and following every spiritual path
and visiting every spiritual teacher.
It wants to become more spiritual.
But if you do happen to stumble upon the truth,
so that there is a very real possibility of your full
awakening, the ego will have you looking
elsewhere almost immediately.
It does not want you to wake up because if you
awaken, it will no longer be in control of you.
It will no longer be in charge.
If the true master appears,
the ego will have to vacate the throne.

The ego is a thief

The ego is a thief.
It wants to steal from you
the truth of Being.
The ego is a politician.
It wants to use the power of Being
to gain an advantage for itself.
The ego is an imposter.
It wants to be the one who knows.
It wants to pose as You.

No judgment

I have no judgment of the ego.
I do not reject the ego in any way.
I am simply commenting on the nature of the ego
based upon what I have observed.

Ego cannot live the truth of Being.

Ego cannot live the truth of Being.
Ego and Being exist within different dimensions.
Ego exists within the human mind.
It exists in the past and the future.
It exists within separation.
Being exists within the present moment.
It exists in Oneness.
It exists as Love.
Ego and Being live according to different laws.
We have gone terribly astray because we have
tried to make the ego live the truth of Being.
It is unfair to ask that of the ego.
It is not meant to be other than what it is.
It exists within duality.
It cannot avoid the negative.
It must exist on both sides of duality.
The most that can be accomplished at the level
of ego is a state of balance within duality.
This opens the doorway to Being.
It opens the doorway to the One.
Religions are an attempt on the part of the
collective mind or ego to practice the truth of Being.
Christianity is that part of the collective mind
seeking to practice the truth of Christ.
Buddhism is that part of the collective mind
seeking to practice the truth of Buddha.

Ego cannot live the truth of Being ....

Islam is that part of the collective mind
seeking to practice the truth of Mohammed.
Religions must fail simply because mind
cannot practice the truth of Being.
Ego must be released from unrealistic expectations.
It is by its very nature separate and fearful.
It is controlling, manipulative and self serving.
It is not unconditionally loving and accepting.
It does not know the truth.
It cannot directly encounter God.
It is limited to the world of belief.
It is what it is.
It is a complete violation of the ego
to try to make it what it is not.
It puts too much pressure on the ego.
It forces the ego into failure and shame.
It feels judged and condemned.
It feels inadequate and insignificant.
And then, in desperation, it rebels.
It tries to make itself bigger than it actually is.
If you judge the ego or reject it in any way,
then it will take you over.
It will control you.
It will assume power over you.

Ego cannot live the truth of Being ....

It will claim you as its own.
Ego cannot live the truth of Being.
It is not supposed to.
If you want to live the truth of being,
then you will have to awaken out of the realm
of the ego into the dimension of Being.
You will have to learn how to be fully present.
You will have to learn how to be in right relationship
with the ego and its thoughts, beliefs and emotions.
You will have to learn the art of
unconditional love and acceptance.
As you love and accept yourself at the level of mind,
and as you awaken into Being, your mind will
gradually be brought into a state of balance.
The ego will be brought to a place of trust and
surrender. And then you will be free.
You will be an awakened Being.
Your mind will be your loving and devoted
servant, just as you will be a loving
and devoted servant of God.
And there will be periods of time in your life
when everything dissolves into perfect blissful
silence. Even your relationship with God dissolves.
You have entered into Oneness with God.
You have entered into the Ocean of Eternity.

The Father, Son and Holy Ghost

At the level of mind, you are the Son.
At the level of Being, you are the Father.
And beyond the Father and the Son
is the Holy Ghost.
Eternal Presence.
God the One.
I am that I am.

Until the ego is surrendered,
you are the prodigal son.

The ego is you from the past
insisting that it is you now.

The ego

Your ego exists within thought.
Thought is its very structure.
The more fixed your thought,
the more rigid your ego.

The wings of thought

Riding on the wings of thought,
you enter the world of time.
Riding on the wings of thought,
you enter the world of the mind.

The ego

The ego will tempt you.
The ego will test you.
The ego will trick you.
The ego will do whatever is necessary
to prevent your escape from the mind.
It is not that the ego is evil.
Keeping you imprisoned within the mind
is the ego's service to God.
After all, your entry into the separation
was a part of your service to God.
It is only by entering into separation
that Oneness can be experienced.
The ego is meant to keep you in the separation.
The ego is the custodian of the separation.

The ego's temptation

It is not difficult for the ego to tempt you.
You fall into temptation over and over again.
All that the ego has to do is offer you the promise
of future fulfillment and you belong to it.
You are caught in the mind.
You are lost in illusion.
As long as you allow yourself to be seduced
by the ego's promise of future fulfillment,
you will never awaken out of the mind's world
of the past and future into the real world
of the present moment.

Temptation

The ego has an infinite capacity
to tempt you away from the present moment.
The ego can tempt you
with the promise of future fulfillment.
The ego can tempt you with the
knowledge of things past.
The ego can tempt you with
the thought of things to come.
How can God compete with that?
God's world is limited to that which is here now.
You cannot make use of that which is here now.
It cannot advance you in any way.
So who will choose God's world?
Who will be able to resist the
temptation of mind's world?
Not many. Only a blessed few.

God's test

If you are willing to be fully present,
then gradually the deeper level of God's world
will be revealed to you.
The hidden treasures will be revealed.
At first, it will not seem like much.
There will be nothing in it for you.
You cannot make use of it in any way.
But that is God's test.
Will you be present even though
there is nothing in it for you?
Will you be present for God's sake
and not for your sake?
Will you honor God and God's world
with your presence?
Will you be present with God?
Will you be present for God?

Is this moment enough?

God has nothing more to offer you
than that which is present in the moment.
Is it enough for you?
God wants to know!
Because if it is not enough for you, then
you will have to leave the present moment.
You will have to enter the illusory world of
the mind in search of something more.

The Quest

A man was searching for the key to happiness.
One day he came upon a sage sitting
by the side of the road.
"Where can I find happiness?" asked the man.
"It is here," answered the sage.
The man looked around.
"But there is nothing here," he said.
"There is nothing here," answered the sage,
"because you are not here. How can you know what
is here if you are not here?"
The man looked confused.
"Become fully present with the trees," said the sage.
"Become fully present with the flowers
and the birds and the distant mountain."
Guided by the sage, the man was able to bring
himself fully present, and as he did so,
everything began to change. The trees became
vibrant and alive. They were full of light.
They seemed eternal. The flowers exploded
into all the colors of the rainbow.
The song of the birds filled the man's ears.
He could feel the soft caress of the breeze
upon his face, and he was warmed gently
by the sun. He began to feel extremely calm
and peaceful. His mind was completely still.
Not a single thought arose.

The Quest ....

He felt love arising within him.
He felt a sense of oneness and perfection.
He was in ecstasy and bliss.
A sense of inner knowing filled him
and at last he was at peace.
For the first time in his life he felt full within.
And he was very, very happy.
Just then he heard a voice inside of him.
It was the voice of his mind.
It was the voice of his ego.
"Do not listen to this foolish old man!" said the
voice. "What can he offer you? Just a few trees,
some flowers and the distant mountain. That is
nothing. I can offer you so much more. I can offer
you everything. All you have to do is think, and it is
yours. All you have to do is imagine and I will take
you there. I can promise you all the treasures of the
world. I can promise you fame and power and glory.
Ask this so-called sage if he can offer you that?"
The sage shook his head.
"I can offer you all the knowledge of the past," said
the voice. "Ask the sage if he can offer you that."
The sage shook his head.
"I can promise you a better future," said the voice.
"Ask the sage if he can do that!"

The Quest ....

The sage shook his head.
"I can bring you everything that is missing
in your life. I can fix up everything that is wrong.
Ask the sage if he can do that!"
The sage shook his head.
The man had heard enough.
"What can you offer me?" he asked the sage.
"Only what is present in this moment,"
answered the sage.
"Is that all?" asked the man.
"Nothing more than that," said the sage.
The man thought for a while.
"No contest!" said the voice triumphantly
inside the man's head. "No contest!"
"There is nothing here," said the man. "Just a few
trees, some flowers and the distant mountain."
With that the man continued on his way, in pursuit
of that which his ego had promised him.
The sage watched as the man disappeared
down the road.
"No contest," said the sage to the trees and the
flowers and the distant mountain.
"No contest."

The present moment

The present moment is always
calling for your attention.
Just look and you will see.
Each leaf moving in the breeze is waving to you.
It is saying, "Here I am.
Will you not be present with me?
Will you not see me?"
Each flower is trying to attract you
with its color and its beauty.
"What more can I do?" asks the flower.
"Will you not see me?
Will you not be present with me.
Do you not know who I am.
I am God in the form of a flower.
And I am trying to attract your attention."

God is without judgment.
The original sin is judgment.

Judgment

As long as you continue to judge,
you will be denied entry into God's world,
not because you have done anything wrong,
and not because you are evil,
but simply because judgment
is incompatible with the true nature of God.

Adam and Eve

In Genesis, we are told that Adam and Eve
were ejected from the Garden of Eden
because they had eaten of the fruit of the tree
of knowledge of what is good and evil.
To decide what is good and evil is a judgment.
It is judgment that resulted in the ejection
of Adam and Eve from the Garden of Eden.
It is judgment that prevents their return.
God had warned them against judgment.
Now judgment had taken them into the world
of duality. It had taken them out of the Mind of
God into a world of their own minds.
They had chosen to separate from God
and go their own way.
Now they are condemned to live
in a world of their own creation.
Adam and Eve exist within each one of us.
It is a story that reflects our original state
of consciousness.
It reflects our original state of Being.
We began in the Garden of Eden.
We began in a state of innocence.
We began in the Mind of God.
Now we are separated from God.
We are fallen from God and the only thing that
keeps us fallen is our continuing judgment.

Adam and Eve ....

When we come to recognize that judgment
is the original sin that led us astray,
we can begin the long and delicate process
of transcending judgment in our lives.
When we have transcended judgment completely,
we will find that we have been restored to God.
We have been returned to the Garden of Eden.
We have found our way home.
But to our utter amazement,
we will find that the Garden of Eden
no longer exists within the mind of God.
That which began as an image in the mind of God
has been manifested into physical form.
The Mind of God has given birth
to the Body of God.
The Garden of Eden
now exists in physical form.
It is our planet Earth.
When we awaken fully into the present moment,
we will realize that we have come home.
In fact, we have always been home.
But like Adam and Eve, we have abandoned God
and the Garden of Eden by journeying into
the illusory world of our own minds.

Beyond judgment

The only way to go beyond judgment
is to witness yourself judging.
Do not try to stop judgment,
for that too would be a judgment.
It would be a judgment of judgment.
Just see judgment as it arises within you.
Own it.
Confess it.
Express it.
Allow judgment to exist within you
but do not believe in it.
Judgment is waiting to be accepted.
It is the final test.
Once you pass the test,
judgment will release you.
If you want to go beyond judgment,
then you will have to get to know judgment.
Know yourself as the one who judges.

Beyond judgment ....

Know yourself as the one who is judged.
Witness judgment in its many forms.
Witness judgment in its many disguises.
Witness judgment each time it arises in your life.
Just say to judgment as it arises within you,
"I see you judgment. I acknowledge you.
I don't judge you, reject you or deny you in any way.
I simply don't believe in you any more.
I no longer choose to judge anyone or anything.
But thank you for letting me see you so clearly
whenever you arise within me. I love you."
As you come to know judgment, and as you accept
it without judgment, it will begin to dissolve.
It will disappear from your life completely.
You will experience a life without judgment.
You will open into love.
You will awaken into the truth of life.
You will be restored into Oneness with God.

Trust in God

So many souls have entered into separation
from God because their trust in God
was not unconditional.
They turned away from God in times of suffering.
This is a judgment against God and it is judgment
that leads us into separation.
How can we know God's design in the
unfolding drama of human existence?
When I speak of God,
I am not speaking of a God outside of you
or some entity in some far distant Heaven.
God is much closer than that.
God is everything.
Everything is God.
This very moment is God.
Everything happening in this moment is God.
God is constantly unfolding and revealing
God's self, moment to moment.
Whatever is happening in this moment
is the will of God,
simply because it is happening.
To reject what is happening in any moment
is to be against the will of God.

Trust in God ....

And when you resist the will of God,
you create your own suffering.
We are meant to live our lives surrendered
to the will of God.
I am not speaking of conditional trust
or conditional surrender.
It has to be unconditional.
You cannot say to God,
"I trust you and I am surrendered to your will
as long as things go my way."
If you do that, God will bring into your life all sorts
of things that you do not want, not to punish you
but to give you the opportunity to accept what is
happening. It is only this level of acceptance that
will bring you home because it is only at this level of
acceptance that judgment within you is transcended.
God will never give up on you.
Everything that happens in your life provides you
with that opportunity of unconditional surrender.
You are not surrendering to suffering.

Trust in God ....

You are surrendering to whatever is happening
in your life, even if that involves the death
of your loved ones.
It is your refusal to accept
what is happening that creates your suffering.
I am not suggesting that you should not feel grief
at the loss of loved ones.
If hurt, sorrow and a sense of loss arise
within you, then feel your feelings fully.
Those feelings are a part of the present moment.
But if you go through the experience with a genuine
attitude of acceptance, you will not suffer.
There is no reason why death cannot
be an occasion for celebration.
After all, death is nothing more than a transition.
As long as your will is at variance with the will
of God, then you are creating separation.
You are removing yourself from
Oneness with God. And Oneness with God
is your true home where there is no suffering.

Acceptance

To trust in God really means to live
in total acceptance of what is.
This does not mean that you live passively
in the world. You live in the world with love,
honesty and integrity. You live an empowered life
in partnership with God.
You know that your experience of life
depends entirely upon the choices you make.
You know that your thoughts, words and actions
lead inevitably to the consequences that follow.
You know clearly what you want and what you do
not want but you are not attached to the outcome.
If things do not go your way, then you trust that
whatever is happening is exactly what is meant
to be happening for your highest good and for
the highest good of all. Perhaps you were not fully
conscious in your choices or in your thoughts,
words and actions.
Perhaps God has a lesson for you that will later
prove to be invaluable, even if you can not see its
value right now. Perhaps God has a grander plan
for you than you have for yourself.
In any event, your trust in the unfolding will of God
is unwavering and unshakable. If it is happening, it
must be the will of God. If you do not accept what
is happening, then you have entered into judgment,
which will take you into separation. It is that simple.

Trust in God

Every leaf falling from every tree
is falling at exactly the time
and in exactly the way
that God planned.
Watch a leaf fall.
Its journey to the ground
has been planned by God
in perfect detail.
Every movement in the wind,
every change in direction,
every floating,
flying
falling
movement
is pre-determined by God
in perfect detail
long before
the tree
itself
came
into
existence.
If God has such a perfect plan
for the journey of a leaf from a tree,
how much more perfect is God's plan for you.

Competing with God

At the level of ego,
we are competing with God as the Creator.
At a deeply unconscious level,
the ego wants to be God.
Ego is seeking to empower itself
in its own creation.
All of our philosophical and scientific structures
are creations of ego attempting to compete
with God as the one who knows.
Philosophy is knowledge competing with knowing.
Science is knowledge competing with truth.
There is no innocence in philosophy.
There is no innocence in science.
It is a part of the ego's need to be in control.
When you compete with God,
you separate yourself from God.
If you give up competing with God
as the Creator, you will be able to participate
with God in God's creation.

What is God to do?

So many people on the planet are lost
in the world of the thinking mind.
They are asleep, dreaming that they are awake.
So what is God to do?
We are so destructive in our ignorance
and our unconsciousness that we are
on the brink of destroying ourselves.
What will it take to wake us up out of illusion?
Many prophets and sages and masters have tried.
But to what avail?
Perhaps we have left God with no alternative
but to shake us up. Perhaps it is only when life
becomes so painful and uncomfortable
that we will stop long enough to see
that we are lost in illusion
and that our unconsciousness
is the sole cause of our suffering.

The presence of God

God has already created all that is.
There is nothing you can add to it
nor is there anything you can take away.
God's world exists here now.
By bringing yourself fully present,
you will be able to participate in it.
You will be able to experience it.
The tree and the flower and the rock
are a part of God's world.
Indeed, they are a part of the body of God.
By bringing yourself fully present
with the tree or the flower or the rock,
you bring yourself into God's world.
God has already done God's part.
Now it is up to you to do your part.
Your role is vital.
Bring yourself into the present moment.
Be fully present with that which
is actually here now.
By becoming fully present you will begin
to awaken out of the illusion of separation
into the truth of life.
By becoming fully present, you will begin to
encounter the living Presence of God
in all things present.

Everyone is God

I was walking along a crowded city street one day,
when I became aware that everyone I saw
seemed to be a fully awakened Being.
Everyone I saw appeared to be God-realized.
Everyone I saw was God.
Even the beggar by the side of the road looked
very much like God pretending to be a beggar.
It occurred to me that everyone
had always been awake and God-realized
and that I was the last to arrive.
I was the last to awaken.
It was a humbling experience.

Giving it back to God

A woman came to an introductory gathering
one warm summer's night in August.
At the end of the evening, she approached me
and introduced herself as Margaret.
She said that she had experienced a very powerful
awakening towards the end of the evening. She said
that she was feeling very expanded and present.
She seemed to be in a very blissful state.
She had never experienced anything like this before
and so she asked me how to live in this expanded
state of consciousness.
I told her to just relax and enjoy it.
Several days later she telephoned to thank me.
She said that what she had experienced that night
was continuing for her and that she had never had
such a wonderful few days.
She was in a state of profound love, experiencing
beauty and perfection in everything.
She had been feeling very happy and very blissful.
I was pleased for her and a little surprised
as she explained that she was an absolute
beginner and had never attended any
spiritual classes or workshops before.
The following day, I went off to run a three
day residential retreat. After the retreat,
I returned to the home of my hosts.

Giving it back to God ....

It was about eleven thirty in the evening when I
arrived home and I found an urgent telephone
message on the desk in my room.
It was from Margaret.
"Please call if you get in before midnight," it read.
I dialed the number on the note and Margaret
answered the phone. She sounded distressed.
"How could you be so cruel?" she said.
I asked her what she was talking about.
"How can you do this to people?" she continued.
I had no idea what she was talking about,
so I asked her to explain.
"How can you give such a gift to people and not
tell them that it will go away. How can you show
someone what life can be like without a warning
that it does not last."
Her tone was very accusatory.
She had gone very deeply into blaming me
for whatever she was experiencing now.
"What are you actually experiencing?" I asked her.
"Well, I have been so happy for about a week
now," she explained. "I have never felt so much
love and laughter and joy and then it suddenly
went away. And now I am full of despair. It would
have been better to have not known the heights of
joy, because now I am in the depths of despair."

Giving it back to God ....

"Would you like some guidance?" I asked her.
"Yes!" she replied with a little hesitation.
"If I offer you guidance," I insisted, "then you will
have to do exactly as I say!" She agreed.
"Very well," I continued. "When you go to bed
tonight, I want you to close your eyes and become
very present in your breathing body. I want you to
experience the silence within, even if it is only for a
few moments. And then I want you to speak into
the silence. I want you to apologize to God."
"What am I apologizing for?" she asked with
considerable surprise.
"Apologize to God for trying to hold on to
something which does not belong to you," I
answered. "God has given you an amazing gift.
God has given you a glimpse of who you really are.
God has revealed to you the truth of life and love.
Now apologize to God for being ungrateful.
Apologize to God for trying to keep it all for
yourself. I want you to say these words to God.
I give it all back to you, God. The love and the
truth and the bliss belong to You and to the present
moment. These gifts are only available to me when
I am in the present moment. Through Your grace,
you have shared these things with me,
but they are not mine to keep.

Giving it back to God ....

They belong to You and to You alone. I am very
grateful but now, I give it all back to You."
There was a long pause before she spoke.
"I don't think I can do it," she said.
"What if it never comes back!"
I reassured her that she could do it or that she
could at least try to the very best of her ability.
She agreed to try.
I was exhausted when I finally got to bed.
At exactly nine o'clock the next morning,
the phone rang. It was Margaret.
"Thank you! Thank you! Thank you!," she enthused.
"What are you thanking me for?" I asked.
"I did exactly as you suggested," she said.
"I apologized to God. I gave all the love and the
happiness and the joy back to God. Then I went
to sleep. When I woke up this morning, it was all
back and I felt so full of love and peace and
gratitude. It is much quieter than it was before
but it is basically the same feeling."
We spoke for a little while longer.
After I had hung up the phone, I closed my eyes
and entered into a deep and silent prayer of
gratitude. I gave thanks to God
for this valuable lesson.

Remembering God

If you remember God and live in conscious
awareness of the presence of God in all things
present, then your creative efforts will be in total
harmony with God's creation.
You will not be competing with God.
You will not create anything that conflicts
with God's creation.
You will not create anything
that is harmful or toxic to God's creation.
You will not create anything that detracts from the
natural beauty and glory of God's creation.
In fact, your contribution will add
to the beauty of God's world.

Living in two worlds

Many people are afraid to awaken
because they believe that if they awaken fully
they will no longer be able to function in the world.
There is a certain level of enlightenment
where this is true.
Every now and then, I enter into a state
where I am outside of time.
There is absolutely no sense of myself
outside of the moment.
There is no memory of myself in the past
and no sense of myself in the future.
All separation dissolves as I enter
into the Oneness of Now.
It is an experience of Heaven on Earth,
which is exquisite beyond imagining.
But at this level of consciousness,
it is impossible to live in the world of time.
There is no way to engage in anything
outside of the moment.
If you were to remain in that state, you would
need a team of caretakers to take care of you.
And so I recommend a softer version
of enlightenment.
One which allows for the world of time
to gently co-exist with the timeless world of Now.

Living in two worlds ....

There is no reason why we cannot
bring these worlds into balance and harmony.
Learn the art of living in the moment.
Awaken and deepen into Being.
Become thoroughly grounded in Being.
Have profound experiences of God and Heaven
and Earth as often as God's grace allows,
but do not become attached to those experiences.
Know that the present moment is the truth of life
and that the world of the mind is illusory in nature.
Then you can play in the world of the mind,
as much as you like, but beware!
It is easy to get lost there.
Let God's world of the present moment
be the foundation of your existence.
Only enter into the mind's world of thought,
memory idea, concept, opinion and belief with
conscious intention and never become
so involved that you become lost in it.
Do not become attached to the positive aspects
of life at the level of mind and do not reject
the negative. Do not become caught in desire,
which takes you into the future
or fear which closes you down.

Living in two worlds ....

Do not become identified with your own story
as it unfolds through time.
To become more grounded in Being,
learn the art of being fully present,
not just when you are sitting silently,
but also in your daily activities.
Have your morning shower in Presence.
Walk through the park and be fully present
with the trees and the flowers and the birds.
Eat your meals in Presence, chewing and tasting
each mouthful with love and attention,
appreciating the delicate textures and flavors
of the food you are eating.
You can even wash the dishes in Presence.
The more you remember to be present
the more you will become grounded in Being.
And then, when you do go off into thought
and imagination and the world of ideas,
opinions and beliefs, it will be much easier
for you to return to the real world
of the present moment.
It will be much easier for you
to remain awake in the truth of life.

From mind to Being

In the early stages of awakening,
you will have blissful and profound
experiences of the awakened state of Being,
but you will inevitably return to your mind.
Your mind is the home in which you live.
It is the home to which you have grown accustomed.
Occasionally you will leave your home and visit
the present moment, but you will not be
allowed to remain there.
It is as if there is an imaginary elastic band attached
to you which quickly snaps you out of the present
moment and back into the past and future
world of the mind.
However as you deepen into Being and become
more grounded in the present moment,
and as you bring more of the light of consciousness
to the mind, a gradual shift begins to take place.
The imaginary elastic band becomes stretched and
loosened. You will find yourself spending more and
more of your time in the present moment. The mind
is not so insistent upon your immediate return.

From mind to Being ....

This relaxation and surrender of the mind continues,
until one day, without warning and without notice,
your home has shifted from mind to Being.
Now your home is in the present moment.
To be present is your natural state.
You still enter the mind's world
of the past and future.
You still think.
But when you have finished thinking,
you will spontaneously return to the awakened
state of Being, which is your new home.
The elastic band is now pulling you
in the opposite direction.
It is pulling you from mind to Being.
When this shift occurs, you have passed through
a major transformation in your life.
You are now awake.
You are in your true home.
No more effort is required.

Living in the world of time

As you awaken, you will be confronted
with an important question.
"Now that I am awakening into the truth of life
lived in the present moment, how do I live in a
world where almost everyone is focused on the
past and future? How do I live in a world of fear
and desire when I am no longer ruled by fear and
desire and when I am no longer seduced by the
promise of future fulfillment?"
The answer is simple.
Choose to be present as much as possible.
Only enter into thought with conscious intention.
Feel the presence of God within you
as the source of your strength and power.
Choose love, not fear.
Surrender the will of your ego to a higher dimension
of your Being and honor God and the present
moment above all. Do not follow the urges, cravings
and habits of your ego. It may take a little time to
overcome habitual patterns but if your commitment
is there, it is not difficult. Surrender patterns of
judgment, control and manipulation.

Living in the world of time ....

Be present.
Be responsive in the moment.
Know what you want, moment to moment.
If you are thirsty, drink.
If you are hungry, eat.
If you are lonely, seek out some companionship.
What you want is constantly changing
so do not be attached to the outcome.
Feel your feelings, for they are
good indicators of what you want now.
This is different to the desires of the mind
which involve you in the future and take you
further and further away from the present moment.
They promise fulfillment but they never deliver.
Be present.
Be responsive.
Be authentic.
Feel your feelings.
Know what you want, moment to moment.
It will deliver you through life, constantly renewing
you from one moment to the next.

Feel your feelings

It is very important to feel your feelings.
It is only in physical form that we have the
opportunity to experience life through the
phenomena of feeling. It brings a quality of
richness and vitality to our lives that we cannot
experience in other dimensions of existence.
Feelings carry a life force within them.
They give us a dynamic sense of being alive.
However, there are some fundamental principles
which must be understood, if you are to be in right
relationship with feelings.
Feelings arise in the moment.
They relate to whatever is happening in the moment.
They flow through you.
Once the moment that you are responding to has
passed, then the feelings vanish.
They do not linger. They are not meant to linger.
If you are on a roller coaster ride at an amusement
park, that feeling of excitement and fear as you
descend is immediate. It belongs to that moment
alone. The feeling of joy that arises as you behold
the beauty of the sun setting over the ocean belongs
to that moment alone. The feeling of love that fills
your heart as you gaze into your beloved's eyes
belongs to that moment alone.
The feeling of triumph as you direct a perfect
passing shot past your opponent in a game of

Feel your feelings ....

tennis belongs to that moment alone.
When we are responsive to whatever is happening
in the moment and when we allow ourselves to feel
our feelings fully, we bring vitality and aliveness
into our bodies and into our lives.
Feelings do not belong in the world of time.
It is important not to take them there.
If you become identified with or attached to the
positive feelings like joy or happiness so that you
want to hold onto them, you interrupt their flow
through you. You take them out of the present
moment into the world of time. You take them
into the world of the thinking mind.
You have contaminated feelings with thought.
It is the same if you reject or repress so-called
negative feelings like sadness, hurt or anger as
they arise within you. You have taken those
feelings out of their natural flow and locked
them within you. You have dammed the river
of feelings flowing through you.
They are caught in the world of your mind.
Feelings arising in the moment do not belong to
you. They belong to God or the present moment.
They are simply flowing through you.
Let them flow freely. Express them responsibly.
You will be richly rewarded if you do so.

Feelings and emotions

There is a radical difference between
feelings and emotions. Feelings arise in the
moment and they flow through you.
They are energy in motion.
E-motions are feelings taken out of motion.
They are held within you, both at a memory level
within your mind and at a cellular level within your
body. They consist of positive feelings from your
past which you have become attached to or
identified with and will not let go of
or they are negative feelings which you
have repressed within you.
In either case, you have not allowed these feelings
clear passage through you and so now they are
stuck within you.
They are feelings converted to e-motion.
They are held within you like a finely tuned spring,
which can be activated at the slightest stimulation.

Feelings and emotions ....

Emotions from some past experience can come
flooding in at any time to color the experience
of the present moment, preventing your authentic
response to whatever is happening right now.
Instead, you are caught in the past, reacting
emotionally to your projections from the past.
You are no longer responsive.
You have become reactive.
Most of your problems
are attributable to this simple fact.
You will have to go through a process of releasing
these emotions that are repressed within you.
They are holding you in the past.
They are slowly poisoning you.
Once you have released the emotions
from the past, you can deepen into Presence
and come into right relationship with feelings
as they arise in the moment.

The body of God

Everything around you is the body of God.
Bring yourself fully present.
See it.
Hear it.
Taste, touch and smell it.
Every mountain, every rock
and every grain of sand is the body of God.
Every flower and every leaf
on every tree is the body of God.
Every planet and every distant star
in every universe
is the body of God.
The food you eat,
the water you drink
and the air you breathe
are all of the body of God.
Your own body is the body of God.
Everything in physical existence
is the body of God.
Be here now.
Be present in the body of God.
Be present with the body of God.
Be present as the body of God.

God dwells within me.
I dwell within God.
And we are One.

When you awaken, you are the true Master.
But only of yourself.

The pure consciousness of I AM

The pure consciousness
of I AM
is the bridge between
the Mind of God
and the Body of God.
It is the bridge between
the Father and the Mother.
It is the bridge between
the above and the below,
the inner and the outer
and the beginning and the end.
It is the bridge between Heaven and Earth.
It is the consciousness of Christ.
Awaken now
to the
I AM
that you are.

The eternal nature of God

Creation is constantly giving birth to itself.
Life is the womb of death
and death is the womb of life.
Creation and destruction are dual aspects of God.
That which is born shall die.
That which dies shall be born anew.
That which is created shall be destroyed.
That which is destroyed shall be created anew.
That which begins will end.
And that which ends will begin again.
Such is the eternal nature of God.

In the end is the beginning.

ABOUT THE AUTHOR

Leonard Jacobson is a modern mystic and spiritual teacher who is deeply committed to guiding and supporting others in their journey towards wholeness.

He was born in Melbourne, Australia in 1944. He was educated at the University of Melbourne, graduating in law in 1969. He practiced law until 1979. He then set off on a long journey of spiritual discovery which took him all over the world, from the United States to the Middle East, India, and Japan.

In 1981, he experienced the first of a series of spontaneous mystical awakenings that profoundly altered his perception of life, truth and reality. Each of these experiences took him to deeper and deeper levels of consciousness.

He has been running workshops and seminars for the past sixteen years, offering inspiration and guidance to those on the path of awakening. His teachings and his presence are a powerful reminder that the source of life and truth is within each one of us.

He maintains a home in Byron Bay, on the eastern coast of Australia, although much of his time is now spent in the USA, offering evening gatherings, weekend workshops and longer retreats there.

Leonard Jacobson

To find out when there will be a seminar or retreat
in your local area or to order books and tapes:

In the USA, call 1-888-367-3315 (toll free)

In Australia, write to Leonard Jacobson,
PO Box 434, Byron Bay, NSW 2481, Australia.

Or visit the author's website:
www.leonardjacobson.com

Embracing the Present

Living an Awakened Life

This book casts a bright light upon the path of spiritual awakening. With perfect precision, the author leads the reader through the maze of the mind and its illusory world of the past and future into the real and illumined world of the present moment. To read this simple yet powerful and challenging book is to embark upon a spiritual journey which will touch you deeply and bring fullness and completion into your life.

ISBN 1-890580-01-5, 288 pages
Available from leading book stores.
To order a copy of *Embracing the Present*
call 1-888-367-3315
or visit the authors website at
www.leonardjacobson.com

A Universe of Dancing Stars